JONATHAN RUMBOLD

Children of the Vikings

DRAGON
Granada Publishing

For Thrainn, Solveig, and Alfur, who introduced me to Iceland: and Anita, who insisted upon a *heroine*.

This story is based on an incident recorded in the anonymous Icelandic saga *Hrafnkels saga Freysgoda*. These events took place around the year 998 A.D.

Dragon Books
Granada Publishing Ltd
8 Grafton Street, London W1X 3LA

Published by Dragon Books 1985

First published by Granada Publishing
in hardback 1985

ISBN 0-583-30729-9

Made and printed for
William Collins Sons & Co. Ltd, Glasgow

Set in Plantin

IMPRIMÉ EN FRANCE

Raiders from the Sea

In this year came the forementioned (Viking) host after Easter to East Engle, and they got control of East Engle, and there spent three months attacking and burning. Even into the most desolate parts of the marshes they went, slaughtering men and cattle, and burning everything. Then at last they made their way back to their ships with the plunder that they had taken . . .

The Anglo-Saxon Chronicle

'Make one move and I'll kill you!' the tall Viking barked, pitching the terrified girl head-first into the cargo well at the front of the boat.

Elf lay where she had fallen, sprawled over the keel-timber, with her feet resting in a pool of foul smelling sea water. Out of the corner of her eye she could see that there was another prisoner behind her, sitting huddled into the space beneath the deck. A boy, of about her own age, maybe a little older. Elf tried to get a better look at him, but at that moment some clinking sacks were thrown down into the hold beside her, followed by the bloodstained carcasses of two sheep.

She could hear the Vikings talking on the deck just above her.

'Has your blood turned to milk, Thorfinn Redbeard, that you spare the children of the Saxons?'

'Shut your mouth, you one-eyed troll! I've as much right to the pickings from this trip as any man!'

The men walked away down the deck, still arguing.

Elf had been able to understand what they had been saying, as there were many Norse settlers living near her village, and her best friends had been the children of a Danish farmer. She understood their language almost as well as her own.

Crash!

Elf screamed. The huge anchor, dripping with stinking river mud, had been lowered into the bottom of the boat just beside her.

Boom! *Boom*! *Boom*!

Now the Vikings were ramming the massive pine-trunk oars through the holes in the side of the longship. The vessel gave a sudden lurch, and Elf rolled over into the pool of water which had collected in the bottom. They were leaving. Already she could feel the movement of water beneath the planking of the hull.

Elf struggled up into a sitting position, leaning awkwardly against one of the dead sheep. She looked across at the boy. He was staring at her without moving. His thin, pale face was without expression. All his clothes were torn and dirty, and there was a metal collar around his neck. A rusty chain had been looped around the collar, and padlocked to an iron ring on the hull.

A slave . . . Elf thought. For the first time she understood what was happening to her. She was going to be a slave, like this boy. That was why they hadn't killed her, even though the big red-bearded Viking had meant to at first, when he found her. He had been helping himself to all the silver in the church. Then he had seen her, a small flaxen-haired figure, barefoot, muddy, and trembling, hiding behind the altar.

He had raised his sword to strike her, and then, strangely, he had hesitated. She remembered seeing his eyes looking at her through the slits in his helmet. Cold, blue eyes, that did not seem to blink. They had stared at each other for what had seemed like a very long time. Then the Viking had suddenly sheathed his sword, let out a stream of curses, and hauled her on to his shoulder.

Elf glanced up. The boy was still sitting silently on the other side of the boat, without moving.

'*Specan thu Anglisch*?' she asked him in her own tongue. She thought that he might have been taken, like her, from one of the villages on the coast, although he did not really look like an Angle or a Saxon boy. He was wearing woollen breeches, like the Norsemen, and his tangled hair was so fair that it was almost white.

'Where are they taking us?' Elf persisted, this time talking in Norse, the language of all the Viking peoples. The boy still did not reply.

Up on the rowing deck, the Vikings began to pull on their oars, faster and faster and in perfect time. As they rowed, they howled out the words of a song – a triumphant chant in time with their oar strokes – which seemed to be all about blood, and death, and strange gods. The singing terrified Elf, and she began to cry.

'They killed my mother . . .' Shaking with sobs, she sank her face into the skirt of her tunic. Still the boy said nothing. He did not seem at all interested in his new companion.

'They killed everybody . . .' Elf wailed. The acrid odour of burning reed-thatch lingered in her nostrils, and a smokey smell still hung about the coarse flax-weave of her tunic. She could not forget. She would never forget.

The Vikings had cut down the villagers as they ran from the blazing huts. The old men, the women, all her friends. They had even killed the animals. That was the noise she would always remember, the agonized screeching of the pigs, which had drowned out even the screaming of the children.

And her mother . . .

Her mother screaming for Elf to run. She had hesitated, as two of the Vikings came towards her out of the smoke. Then one of them had raised his axe, and she had started running. But she had seen it, out of the corner of her eye. Seen the flash of the blade and heard her mother screaming.

She tried to forget. Much of what had happened was already a confused blur of noise and terror. She had no idea how she had got to the little wooden church across the marsh, where the red-bearded Viking had found her. And the memories of those happy times, before the Vikings had come, were fading already from her mind. She would remember her homeland now only as she had last seen it: the giant columns of smoke rising into the air from the burning villages; the dying animals and the burning hayfields; and the sun, a pale blood-red disc behind the vast pall of smoke which had covered the sky.

'*One, two, three, heave*!'

Elf looked up, and dried her eyes on the skirt of her tunic. She had cried until there were no more tears left. It was almost dark now. The Vikings had hauled up the mast, and a striped sail now billowed out from the crossbeam. The boy seemed to be asleep already, his head resting on a coil of damp rope.

As the great oak hull shifted and creaked with the motion of the waves, trickles of seawater seeped in between the planking. Elf was shivering from the cold and damp, and after a while she struggled across to the other side of the boat and huddled close to the boy for warmth. She put an arm around his shoulder, and tried to sleep. After a time she realized that he was crying. They squeezed closer together, sharing their misery at last, and in a little while they both slept.

'What's your name?' the boy asked, as he shared out the hunk of dry bread they were given the next morning.

'Aelflida. Most people call me Elf, for short. That's what it means.' They spoke to each other in Norse. 'What's your name?'

'Olaf.'

Elf frowned. 'Are you one of the Norse folk then?' She guessed that he must be. His name was unfamiliar, and he spoke the language fluently, unlike herself. She spoke the Viking tongue with a heavy, sing-song accent, and still got some of the words wrong.

'My father was from Norway,' Olaf told her, 'But we lived in Shetland. On an island. The raiders took me when I was seven. Jomsvikings. They're the worst. They sold me to a shoemaker in Haideby. I've been a slave ever since.'

'Is that what they'll do, sell me?'

The boy nodded. 'When we get back to Danemarc. You'd better pray to your god that you get a kind master . . .'

Elf gnawed hungrily at the hard bread. 'Is he here, on the ship, your master?'

'Who? The shoemaker? No, he's dead. These Vikings got us, I belong to them now. They'll sell me to somebody else. Like you.'

Suddenly the look-out's voice boomed out, 'Sail ahead! Ship ahead on the steerboard side!'

Elf and Olaf looked at each other, wondering what was happening. Elf clambered up on to the deck and peered over the shield rack. To her surprise they were sailing quite close to land. She had imagined that the sea was so immense that it would take weeks and weeks to cross, but now she could see yellow sand dunes stretching away into the distance and beyond that a wooded heathland.

Some way ahead of them another sailing vessel was moving out slowly from behind the farthest line of sand dunes. It seemed to be of a similar type to their own, but as far as Elf could see it was bigger and broader, and did not seem to be moving very fast.

'What's happening?' hissed Olaf, who was unable to climb up beside her because of his chain.

'They've seen another ship.'

The Vikings peered eagerly at the other vessel.

'It's a merchant ship,' said one. 'What do you say, boys – shall we do a little trading with them?' An ugly smile crept across his face and he turned to the shouts and cheers of the crew. As he did so, Elf saw that the man had only one eye. Where the other should have been, there was only a hideous scar.

Then a familiar voice broke through the din. 'How do we know they're not well defended?' It was the red-bearded Viking, Elf's captor. He screwed up his weather-beaten face, and scanned the horizon with an experienced eye.

'Lost your stomach for a fight as well, child-sparer?' sneered One-Eye. He drew his sword and raised it in the air. 'Who says we take her?' he shouted. 'They'll never outrun the *Snake*!' A roar of approval echoed round the longship.

Some men ran to furl the sail, then lowered the great mast to the deck.

'Every man to his oar!' the helmsman shouted.

Elf and Olaf seemed entirely forgotten in the excitement. Elf was so bewildered by the furious activity all around her that she remained standing on the deck, looking around her in panic, unable to think what to do.

'Start rowing!' the helmsman called out, 'and may the Thunder God be with us!'

The Sea Wolves Attack

The gap between the two ships was closing rapidly. Elf craned her neck and could just see the men on the other ship. They were hauling on their sail-ropes, trying to get every ounce of speed out of the wind. But it was no use. The Vikings on the longship were pulling steadily on their oars, and all the time the helmsman beat the end of his spear on the deck, drumming out the pace, faster . . . faster . . .

A helmeted Viking pushed past her and leaped up on to the prow. He was carrying a grappling iron on the end of a very long rope, and had a shield on his back. In the stern, the helmsman adjusted the heavy steering board, bringing the *Snake* on a collision course with the other ship.

The Vikings were reaching for their painted shields.

'What did I tell you, Arnulf One-Eye?' Redbeard called out. 'They're well defended!'

'Save your breath for your rowing, child-sparer, and leave the rest to Thor! Shields up, lads. We're going to have some rain!'

Almost immediately a hail of arrows rose into the air from the other ship, curving through the sky and falling in a shower towards them. Elf threw her arms up to protect her head. The Vikings held their shields above their heads. The arrows clattered on to the canopy of painted shields, rained down on the deck, and embedded themselves in the ship's timbers. Elf kept her eyes tightly shut until the noise stopped. When she opened them again, she saw to her horror that one of the arrows was stuck fast into the thick oak of the hull, only a thumb's breadth away from the top of her head.

'*You! Whelpling!*' Redbeard bellowed from his rowing position. 'Haven't you got any sense in your Saxon head? Get under the deck!'

Elf did not wait to be told again, and ran along the deck. As she scrambled down into the bows, she caught a glimpse of another swarm of arrows coming at them.

Somebody shouted, '*Ship oars!*' There was a roar of triumph from the crew. The longship continued to crash through the spray under its own momentum. On the prow, the serpent's fangs gaped wide, as if the ship itself could smell the blood of its victims.

The Viking on the prow began swinging the grappling iron around his shoulder. Others had already started to throw spears across on to the other ship. The air was thick with war cries.

It looked as if nothing now could stop the *Snake*.

But the crew of the other vessel had manoeuvred side-on to their attackers. Their ship had a massive iron anchor with spiked prongs and, at the very last moment, they lowered it down across their bows and held it there with ropes. Seconds later the front of the *Snake* rammed itself violently on to the prongs. With a terrible splintering sound, one of the pointed arms of the anchor pierced through the longship's hull – right next to where Olaf was crouching.

Elf tried to stand up, but was instantly knocked down again by a huge cascade of sea water. She came up, gasping for air, dazed and confused. Above the noise of rushing water, she heard the sound of metal clanging on metal, shields splintering, bloodcurdling war cries, and shouts of battle. Olaf! Where was he?

'Olaf!' she screamed. He hadn't come up out of the water! She struggled towards the place where he had been. Gropping in the rushing, ice-cold water she at last found him. She grabbed his hair, and managed to get his head above the surface. But his eyes were closed and he didn't seem to be breathing.

He's dead, she thought with horror. Then he opened his mouth, spitting water. She yelled at him, 'Olaf! Get up! You've got to get up out of the water!'

It was nearly up to their waists already. All the time more and more water was gushing in through the hole. Still Olaf made no attempt to pull himself up.

His chain! Despite the swirling water and the confusion, the thought went through Elf like a hot iron. *He's chained up*! *The ship's going to go down and take him with it*!

'Move, Olaf!' she screamed, but the boy made no effort to help himself. Elf grabbed him round the waist. Somehow she managed to push him into a sitting position against the side of the hull. Immediately she began wrenching at his neck collar.

'Help me!' she moaned. 'You've got to get the chain off. If you don't you'll drown!'

Olaf opened his eyes. 'It's no good Elf. You can't open the lock without the key. Leave me. I'm going to die. It doesn't matter.'

'*No you're not*! I'm not going to let you!' She pulled vainly at the chain, but it held fast. *It's no good*, she thought frantically. *It won't come off*. The water was up to Olaf's chest now. What was she going to do? Even as she looked, she could see the water rising towards his chin.

Then she thought, *An iron bar. I'll have to get an iron bar or something and force it . . .*

All around her was a mass of heaving bodies and hacking weapons. A crewman from the *Snake*, hurling his axe around his head, was holding off three attackers who leaped and wheeled around him, stabbing at him with their swords. Elf searched in vain for the crowbar she needed to prise Olaf's chain from the hull. All she could find was a wooden boathook. *It'll have to do*, she thought. She started to run back along the tilting deck, keeping her head down, flinching each time she saw the flash of an axe blade. Somehow she managed to reach the bows safely.

Only Olaf's head was now showing. She jumped down, and splashed her way over to him. 'Keep your head out of the water!' she yelled again. She grabbed the chain, pulling her way along to the end of it. The hole in the side of the hull was getting bigger, and she could feel the swirling current round her legs. It was difficult to keep upright.

The chain was padlocked to an iron ring. This ring had been riveted to the hull by means of an iron fastening, so that her only hope was to get this fastening off the wood. She hooked the metal prong of the boathook into the ring and put all her weight on to the wooden handle.

It snapped.

The handle floated off into the foam. Elf wept in desperation. There was nothing else she could do to save her friend. The ship gave another juddering lurch and tilted over even further. Olaf went right under.

'Olaf!' Elf screamed out. She half swam, half staggered over to him, and got his head up again.

He didn't seem to want to keep his head up.

'Leave me, Elf,' he gasped. 'It's no use. I've had enough.'

Elf clasped his head against her chest. On the deck just

above them one of the defeated Vikings from the *Snake* was struggling for his life against two men with spears. The Viking roared something about Thor, then took the full force of one of the spears in his chest. He gave a groan, and pitched backwards into the water. As he fell his axe flew from his grasp, bounced against the hull and vanished into the seething water.

The axe . . .Quickly she dived down under the foaming water and grabbed the weapon just before it slithered out of reach into the bottom of the boat.

'Hold your head away!' she yelled, pushing Olaf's head to one side.

She hacked at the wood behind the metal fastening, somehow finding a strength that she never knew she possessed.

'It's coming off!' she shrieked at last. The wood was starting to split. Olaf had let his face sink into the water again. Elf hauled him up by the hair.

'*Olaf*!' she yelled at him. '*It's going to come off*! You're going to live!'

Elf gave a wild shout, and smashed the axe into the hull just below the iron fastening. Then she overbalanced and fell into the water. But it had been enough. The timber behind the fastening split like firewood and, although he was still weighted down by the chain, the padlock, and the ring, Olaf floated free.

Elf grabbed him under the arms and she just managed to get him to the deck timbers. They hung on, weak and exhausted.

A bearded face appeared above them. 'There's two bearcubs down here!' the owner of the beard called out. 'One of them's wearing a collar! Looks like a couple of slaves!' He hauled the exhausted pair out of the water and heaved them over the side of the merchant ship.

They lay where they fell, a pool of sea water forming around them.

'There's slaves enough in Iceland,' remarked a big, broad-shouldered man as he walked past them. 'Best get rid of them.' He looked as if he was the sort of man who stood no nonsense from anybody.

'Oh, come on, Hoggvandi,' protested the man who had found them. 'We might get something for them.'

The big man lowered his sack into the storage hold in the middle of the ship. 'You can get a good farmhand in the booths of Thingvellir for twenty ounces as it is. That wouldn't cover the cost of the food they'd eat on the way home, would it, troll-head?'

'Twenty? That's not such a bad price,' their captor said.

The man called Hoggvandi walked across the deck and started to climb back over on to the longboat. The crew of the merchant vessel were trying to salvage as much as they could from the *Snake* before the wreck went down. He paused on the rail, holding on by one of the sail ropes.

'I didn't say we'd *get* twenty, did I? They look half dead to me. We'd probably end up giving them away. Take them up into the stern with the rest.' He cocked his head towards the back of the boat.

Elf glanced round now. She saw that about seven or eight of the Vikings from the *Snake* were still alive. They had been lined up on the afterdeck, where some of the men from the merchant ship were busy stripping them of their weapons and valuables. While this went on, the Vikings stood in silence with proud and scornful expressions on their faces. Among them, Elf noticed, was Redbeard.

Elf and Olaf were hauled to their feet and dragged off to join the rest of the captives.

Elf could not believe that these cheerful-looking young men really meant to do them harm. They looked so different from the battle-scarred pirates who had first captured her. These men, with their neatly trimmed beards and ruddy cheeks, did not look like Vikings at all, but more like the sons of farmers. Nevertheless, two of them were polishing the blades of their swords on the legs of their woollen trousers, and looked as if they meant to use them.

Redbeard stood calmly while one of the men removed his belt, which looked as if it was valuable. The buckle was made of bronze, inlaid with silver dragons and twined snakes. Redbeard had probably stolen it from somebody else. But when the man took hold of the small silver charm which hung around his neck, the Viking suddenly grabbed hold of his wrist.

'Leave that, Icelander,' he hissed sharply, staring the other man in the eye. 'Do you want to anger the Thunder-God before I go to meet him?'

The other man hesitated, then slowly let go of the charm.

Elf was holding tightly to Olaf's arm. Both of them were trembling violently with fear and cold.

'Will they kill us?' Elf whispered to Olaf.

'I don't know,' he replied, without looking at her.

Then one of the men suddenly grabbed Olaf by the arm. 'Hey!' he shouted to the others. 'If we're going to get rid of these two, at least let's have some sport with them first!'

The rest of the crew cheered. Olaf felt his legs give way underneath him. He fell forwards, but the man held him upright with a strong grip.

'What do they mean?' Elf cried in a choked voice. 'What are they going to do?'

Olaf did not reply. This was how his dreams had always ended. This was the nightmare from which he had woken, night after night, as he lay on the floor of the shoemaker's workshop. This was how his brothers and sisters had died, as living target practice for the Vikings' spears and axes.

'Who'll lay me twelve ounces I can't send the brat to *Hel* with one throw?' said the man holding Olaf. He took a short throwing axe from his belt.

'I'll do it,' ventured the big man called Hoggvandi. 'I'll wager you're too slow, Hoskuld Grimsson. Twelve ounces that you can't kill him with the first throw. Dead, mind. Wounding doesn't count.'

'Then give me a count of three.' The other man released his hold on Olaf, and pushed him down the deck.

'No!' Elf screamed. 'No!'

A strong, hairy arm was flung across her throat from behind. She fought to free herself, but the grip tightened and she could not move.

'One!' shouted Hoggvandi.

Hoskuld Grimsson began swinging the axe from one hand to the other. Olaf started to run, but immediately tripped over the heavy chain which hung from his collar, and crashed on to the deck. All the men were cheering and shouting. Many of them called to Olaf to get up and run, for they did not want to see Hoskuld Grimsson win his money that easily. The boy struggled to his feet, but then seemed unable to move, and remained staring at Grimsson as he swung the axe.

'Two!'

'Run Olaf! Run!' Elf's shrill voice rang out over the din, and it seemed to break the spell of fear which had rooted Olaf's feet to the deck. He turned and ran as fast as he was able, dragging the clanking chain behind him.

'Three!'

The shouting and cheering were deafening. Elf was shrieking. Hoskuld Grimsson swung the axe behind him for the last time, and threw it with tremendous force towards Olaf. The boy stumbled into the rigging underneath the sail, and crashed down on to some water barrels. The axe ripped through the sail and embedded itself in the mast. A tremendous din of jeering and catcalling went up from the onlookers.

'You lost, Hoskuld Grimsson,' said Hoggvandi. 'That's twelve ounces you owe me.'

'How could I have hit him?' Grimsson snarled. 'He jumped out of the way.'

'So? I told you, you're too slow.' Hoggvandi turned to the others. 'Who will lay me double for the next one?' Without looking at her, he took hold of Elf by the shoulders. 'Come on, troll-wives, don't hang back. Who'll lay me double?'

'All right, Harvard Hoggvandi,' one of the men agreed. 'I'll lay you twenty-four.' Everybody cheered. 'Dead, not wounded?'

Hoggvandi nodded. Somebody tossed a throwing-axe to him. He caught it neatly. Elf began muttering a prayer in her own language.

'Courage, whelpling!' a voice suddenly shouted from behind her.

'Shut your mouth, Viking!'

It was Thorfinn Redbeard. 'You still belong to me!' he called out to her. 'I shall take you with me over the rainbow bridge and you will serve me in the fields of Asgard.'

'I said silence!' bellowed the man who was guarding him. He struck Thorfinn savagely on the lip, drawing blood. Elf sank her sharp teeth into Hoggvandi's fat wrist. He gave a high-pitched yell, like a pig, and dropped the axe.

'This one's going to fight for its life, is it?' he roared, shaking Elf from him and sending her sprawling on to the deck.

'*One*!' Hoskuld Grimsson called out. He was trying to catch Hoggvandi out by starting the count before he was ready.

Hoggvandi ran to retrieve the axe. Elf scrambled to her feet and began sprinting down the deck.

'*Two!*'

Hoggvandi had the axe now. Elf was running. Hoggvandi swung the axe from one hand to the other. Elf screamed. She tripped on a piece of loose rope and fell heavily.

'*Three!*'

Elf closed her eyes, and waited for the axe to come.

There was nothing but silence. The roaring and cheering had stopped abruptly. Am I dead, am I in heaven, Elf marvelled.

When she dared to open her eyes, she saw no angels and no rainbows. Only the shiny wet deck of the ship. She looked up in bewilderment. Harvard Hoggvandi was struggling violently with a man in a silver helmet and scarlet tunic, whom she had not seen before.

'Let go of me, Kari Peacock!' Hoggvandi shouted. The other man wrenched the axe from his grasp, and sent the heavy Icelander crashing to the deck. All the rest of the men were muttering angrily now, for they did not care to have their sport interrupted.

The man in the scarlet tunic shouted, 'I'll have no children killed on board this ship!' He drew his sword, and held the point at Hoggvandi's throat. 'Get up, Harvard Hoggvandi!' he ordered.

'What right have you to interfere with our sport, Kari Sigurdarson?' Hoggvandi snarled, as he clambered to his feet. 'They're only slaves. It's our right.'

The other retorted, 'This ship sails under the flag of the White *Kristr*. Slaves or free get the same treatment here.'

Elf looked up and, sure enough, a black flag with a white cross on it flew from the mast. What did it mean? The *Kristr* was what the Norsemen called her own God.

'You seem to forget,' continued the man in the scarlet tunic, 'that this ship is the gift of King Olaf Trygvasson, who charged me to help take the faith to Iceland. No man breaks that faith as long as he's aboard.'

'Is that so?' Hoggvandi sneered. 'And you seem to forget, Peacock, that we're all Icelanders here, which means we're all free men. We owe no allegiance to the King of Norway, eh lads?' The rest of the crew roared their agreement, and Hoggvandi smiled defiantly, knowing he had the crew behind him. 'You worship whatever milksop God you choose, Peacock. We serve the Thunder-God, white cross or no white cross. Eh lads? What do you say? *I* say that Kari the Peacock gives himself too many airs, with his fine clothes and his fancy ways. *I* say we get rid of him and sail home under the flag of the hammer!'

The whole crew started shouting at once, making the sign of Thor's hammer with their fists. Several of them drew their swords.

'Stop talking like a pack of fools!' called out the man named Hoskuld Grimsson, trying to make himself heard above the din. 'His father is a chieftan and a priest of Frey. He's too powerful. We kill his son and we'll all be outlawed, the lot of us. And his family won't rest until we're all dead.'

One of the crew shouted out, 'Challenge him, Hoggvandi. Wrestle him, and we'll sail home under the flag of the winner. The outlaw's life is not for me when I get back. I've been too long away from home already.' Rumbles of agreement rose from the crew.

'That suit you, Peacock?' Hoggvandi sneered. 'Your god against mine?' He sounded confident of winning. He was built for wrestling, and looked more than a match for any man.

'If it is to be the water-wrestling,' came the voice from under the silver helmet. Hoggvandi's eyes narrowed. The point of the other man's sword still stroked his throat.

‘On the deck, curse you,’ he grunted.

‘The water.’

Neither man was willing to give in to the other. The crew settled it. They had been deprived of their fun when Kari Sigurdarson had stopped the axe-throwing. They wanted to see some good sport now, and everybody shouted, ‘The water! The water!’ until Hoggvandi, very reluctantly, had to agree.

He knew that if they fought in the sea he would lose the advantage of his huge weight. In the water, the contest became one of skill and endurance alone.

Elf did not really understand what was going to happen, but she knew that her own life, and Olaf’s too, now depended on the man in the silver helmet. She looked round for Olaf, but he was nowhere to be seen. He had hidden himself somewhere in the depths of the ship.

The man they called Kari the Peacock lowered the point of his sword from Hoggvandi’s neck. He was obviously nicknamed ‘the Peacock’ because of his taste for scarlet tunics and costly fur cloaks. ‘If I win,’ he now called out, ‘every man here will swear to the faith of the White *Kristr*. Agreed?’

Most of the crew nodded. They already worshipped Odin, his son Thor, and a host of other gods and goddesses. What was one more? ‘Agreed, agreed,’ they shouted. Hoggvandi raised his fist.

‘And if he loses,’ he cried, ‘we finish our sport with the slaves, and sail home under the hammer of Thor!’

‘Thor, *heill*! Thor, *heill*! Thor, *heill*!’ The men rammed their clenched fists together in the sign of the hammer.

Hoggvandi began stripping off his leather armour,

boots, and sword belt. 'You married, Peacock?' he enquired in a scornful tone.

The other man undid his cloak fastening. 'I hope to be. When I return.'

'Then your girl will wait for ever, Peacock, for the only thing you will be kissing is the seaweed at the bottom of this Danish sea.' The crew cheered wildly at this remark. Hoggvandi shook his clenched fists in the air, as if he had already won the contest. The other man ignored him, and quietly removed his own boots and armour.

'We shall see,' he said, and lifted off his helmet. Elf was standing quite close to him and, without thinking, she immediately went down on her knees in front of him. He was quite a young man and unlike most of the Vikings he had darkish hair and beard, and his eyes were not blue, but brown.

'Are you a great lord, Master?' she asked him in an awestruck manner. The young man turned, very surprised, and gave a wry smile.

'No, I am not a lord,' he answered. 'We have no lords in Iceland.'

Elf stood up. 'Will I go there, *Aetheling*?'

'If I come out best in this fight, little slave, then you will go there.' He unbuckled his sword belt, and let it drop on to the deck.

Kari looked at her, and smiled. 'I must fight now for what I believe. You understand that? They will kill you if I lose. But I will do my best for you, I promise.'

'You will not lose, *Aetheling*.'

Kari peered closely into her face, then he slowly reached out and touched her forehead. 'You have the Luck,' he said, 'I can see it in your face. There, now I have taken some of it, too.'

'Ready?' Hoskuld Grimsson called out to the two

challengers. Dressed only in their tunics and breeches, Kari and Hoggvandi walked across to the seaward side of the ship. Then both of them bowed their heads for a moment to pray to their respective gods. Elf felt the excitement in the air, for it was as if Thor himself and the White *Kristr* were about to fight, and not two men.

Hoggvandi held out the little hammer charm which he wore around his neck, and howled out a stream of blood-curdling oaths to the sky. Kari raised the silver cross he wore around his neck to his lips, then he turned and looked towards Elf for a moment, and she smiled at him.

All the men rushed over to the side of the ship to watch the contest. Hoggvandi and Kari climbed on to the shield-rail, and everybody immediately began cheering and shouting.

I have to watch, Elf thought. *I have to.* She limped across the deck, and managed to squeeze in between two of the Icelanders without being noticed.

Hoskuld Grimsson raised his hand in the air. He turned to Hoggvandi and Kari. Both nodded. Grimsson gave the signal, and the two men dived into the sea.

Please let him win, please, Elf murmured over and over again. She could not really make out what was happening. Both men had gone under in a swirl of bubbles. Kari's head surfaced first, but almost immediately Hoggvandi appeared behind him, and caught hold of the younger man's head in a savage grip. They struggled and splashed for a moment. Then Hoggvandi wrenched Kari backwards by the hair and pulled his head under the water.

Elf caught her breath. *He's trying to drown him*, she thought. All she could see was arms and legs thrashing about in the water. Then she just made out the dark outline of Kari's body as he dived deep beneath the waves.

'Thor! Thor! Thor! Thor!' the men shouted, pounding their fists together.

'Kristr! Kristr! Kristr!' Elf cried, making the sign of the cross.

Hoggvandi was treading water now, and looking around furiously – trying to guess where his opponent would surface. Then quite suddenly his head disappeared under the waves, and did not come up again.

Elf drew in her breath, and clutched her cheeks. *What was happening down there?* Kari must have got hold of Hoggvandi from below, and pulled him under. But how long could he himself stay under without breathing?

The cheering and shouting were deafening. Both men had been under for what seemed an impossible time.

They've drowned, Elf thought. *They've both drowned.* Then she saw bubbles. One of them was coming up . . .

A head broke the surface. Elf gasped, and closed her eyes in despair. It was Hoggvandi.

Hoggvandi, panting for air and treading water. Hoggvandi smiling, and raising his arms above his head. Hoggvandi making the sign of Thor. There was a roar of applause.

Then, without warning, Kari shot up out of the water and got his arm around the other man's neck.

The crew gasped in astonishment.

Elf opened her eyes. *Kari was still alive. Alive and fighting.*

He took in some massive gulps of air, then managed to get Hoggvandi's head under the water again. The crew were groaning now, and cursing. 'Come on, Hoggvandi!' they shouted. 'Get hold of his head!'

Elf was shouting at the top of her voice too. 'Kari!

Kari! Kari!' she yelled, hoping he would hear her. Perhaps he did, for the crew had gone quiet just at that moment, and her voice was shrill and piercing.

The men renewed their noisy clamour, and Hoggvandi managed to get his head up above the surface of the water. But Kari hung on, and kept his arm locked around the other man's neck in an iron grip. Hoggvandi got his arms free and leaned back, kicking and splashing, trying to get a grip on Kari's chin. The crew cheered wildly. Still Kari hung on. Then both men went down again, and in the splashing and confusion it was impossible to tell which man had the advantage over the other.

Elf peered into the murky green water, and tried to see what was happening. *Please don't let him die*, she prayed. *Please . . .*

A long time went by. There was still no trace of the wrestlers. No bubbles, no shadows in the water, nothing. No clue as to whether they were alive or dead. Eventually all the shouting died away, and everybody stared at the surface of the water in silence.

They've drowned this time, Elf thought. They had already been under for longer than it took to say twenty 'Hail Marys'. *Nobody can go without breathing for that long*, Elf decided.

Even the seagulls reckoned that the disturbance must be over, and swooped down once more over the patch of water where the men had been fighting.

Hoskuld Grimsson turned to the others. 'They're gone, lads,' he muttered. 'This has been a bad morning's work we've done here. We'd best head back to Danemarc. There'll be no welcome for us in Iceland after this.'

'We sail for Iceland,' a voice said from behind him.

Thor Vanquished

It was Kari.

Everybody turned, startled. He had hauled himself up over the shield-rail on the opposite side of the ship. The two wrestlers must have continued their struggle right underneath the hull, and Kari at least had come up on the other side.

'Fetch Hoggvandi out,' Kari choked, then sank to his knees, coughing and spluttering for air. Several men rushed across the deck to look for their crewmate. Elf alone ran to Kari.

'You won, *Aetheling*, you won!' She flung her arms around his neck. Kari was unable to reply for a moment. He coughed, and retched seawater, and took in great gulps of air.

Then at last he said, 'I won, little slave. You shall see Iceland.'

'Did you hear me shouting for you?'

Kari nodded, coughed again, and smiled. 'I heard you . . .'

Hoggvandi was floating in the water on the far side of the sinking longship. He was still alive, but too exhausted to move. Some of the men hauled him in with boathooks, and somehow managed to heave his dripping bulk up on to the deck. Hoggvandi knew he had lost, and made no attempt to get up. He just lay there, face down, coughing sea water.

Kari stood up, steadying himself for a moment on Elf's

shoulder. Then he walked slowly across the deck, and stood looking down at the figure of his defeated adversary. The rest of the crew watched in silence. With a contemptuous gesture, Kari rolled Hoggvandi over with his foot.

'Give me a sword,' he commanded. There was a murmur of surprise. Kari clicked his fingers, and one of the men handed him a sword. He held the blade at Hoggvandi's throat. Hoggvandi groaned, unable to rise. Kari made a quick slice with the blade of the sword.

The men let out a gasp of horror. But instead of cutting the man's throat, Kari had sliced the cord which was tied around his neck and the silver hammer-charm dropped to the deck. Kari picked it up. Then, with a wry smile, he summoned up all his remaining strength and hurled the silver necklet far out into the sea.

'The White *Kristr* has triumphed!' Kari shouted. He held his own silver cross high above his head. 'Now you will accept baptism into the faith, according to your oath!'

The crew muttered amongst themselves, but they knew they had no alternative. They had sworn to take the new faith if Kari won, and oath-breaking they considered the worst of all crimes.

'Fetch me sweet water,' Kari said. Two of the Icelanders rolled up a barrel of drinking water.

'We have no priest so I must baptise you myself,' said Kari. 'This man first.' Once again he rolled over the dripping body of Harvard Hoggvandi with his foot. Hoggvandi groaned, then sat up, and spat on to the deck.

'Curse you, Kari Sigurdarson,' Hoggvandi muttered, as he crouched before his vanquisher.

'I baptise you in the name of the Father, Son, and Holy Ghost. Amen,' Kari said and splashed holy water into Hoggvandi's face. The huge Icelander shook the water out of his beard, and spat noisily.

'Curse you . . .' he repeated. 'What's he going to do for us, this *Kristr*? Will he keep our ship safe in a storm, like Thor, or make us rich like Frey?'

'Next man!' Kari shouted cheerfully, ignoring him.

Kari seemed very pleased by the morning's work. 'Those men there,' he said, indicating the surviving prisoners from the longship, who were still patiently awaiting their deaths. 'I want to show them that the *Kristr* is a merciful God. If they too will accept the baptism, I will spare their lives. Tell them. If they do this I will put them ashore unharmed.'

One of the Vikings stepped forward. 'I'll do it,' he said. 'It's all the same to me.' The battle-scarred warriors from the *Snake* had long ago ceased to believe in any god save gold and silver. They would swear to whatever faith Kari commanded them, so long as it meant saving their skins for another season's raiding. The Viking walked up to Kari, and raised his right hand in the air.

'My name is Ragnar Eiriksson,' he began solemnly, 'and I hereby swear that the great God Thor has no more brains than a pig. Is that enough for you, Icelander? Or do you want me to kiss your breeches as well?'

'I baptise you in the name of the Father, Son, and Holy Ghost,' said Kari, ignoring the raucous laughter of the other Vikings.

'Any my name is Thorgils Gudmundson,' bellowed a second man, almost weeping with laughter. 'And I say that Freyja the daughter of Njord is a fat sow.' His companions exploded with laughter, clutching their sides and reeling around the deck.

Realising that they were making a fool of him and mocking his God, Kari's face had darkened with anger.

He strode over to Thorfinn Redbeard, who alone had refused to come forward and be baptised.

'And you, Viking? Will you renounce your god, and take the baptism?' To his surprise, Thorfinn shook his head.

'I will not, Icelander. Not for you nor for any man. I will not dishonour my god to save my own skin. I accept whatever fate Thor has decided for me.'

Kari looked rather taken aback. 'So be it, Viking. I have offered you mercy, and you have refused it. Are you sure you do not want to change your mind?'

In answer, Thorfinn clenched his fists, and made the sign of the hammer, in readiness for his journey to that far-off country he called Asgard, the dwelling place of the gods. He closed his eyes for a moment, mumbled a few words, then nodded to signify he was ready. Kari took hold of Thorfinn's tunic, and held the blade of his sword against the Viking's chest.

'Farewell, pirate,' he muttered. Thorfinn stared unflinchingly in front of him.

Then a voice shrieked, '*Don't kill him! Please don't kill him!*' Elf had thrown herself in front of them. 'Please *Aetheling*, please Master, he could have killed me when he found me but he didn't hurt me, not once. Please don't kill him . . .' Her voice trailed off.

Kari was still angry. 'Do not try and interfere in things you do not understand, little slave. I swore to spare him if he took the faith. He chose death. It is his right.'

Nobody moved. Nobody made a sound. Thorfinn himself continued to stare into the far distance, without moving.

Kari frowned, as if struggling with his own thoughts. Then his expression softened, and for the second time he reached out and touched Elf's forehead. Then he turned to Thorfinn.

'Is it true you spared the life of this child?'

Thorfinn seemed very taken aback by this question, as if Kari had accused him of some secret crime. Robbing and killing were a way of life for the Vikings but sparing the lives of Saxons was a very shameful thing for a Viking to admit to, especially in public like this.

'I . . . wanted to sell the thing, that's all,' he said, trying to sound as offhand as he could. 'Now be quick with your sword. I am not afraid to die.' He stood straight and tall, his shoulders squared for he knew that the eyes of the crew were on him. Nothing was more important in the life of a Viking than the manner in which he left it.

Elf looked up at Thorfinn, her eyes brimming with tears. 'You said you'd take me with you to the fields of Asgard. You said so.'

Thorfinn, who had been staring in front of him determinedly, caught her eye for an instant, then immediately lowered his head, as if he were overcome with grief or shame.

'Mother of Loki, don't look at me like that, whelpling,' he muttered. At last he raised his head and turned to Kari. 'I could not kill her, that's all,' he said quietly. 'Don't ask me why. Perhaps the whelp put a spell on me. They say they have strange powers, the Saxons. Now kill me, curse you. I have been shamed in the hour of my going, but I want to make a good death, and Thor will forgive me for my weakness.'

Kari stared at him for a moment, then turned to the others. 'This man is to be made a full member of our crew, with full rights.'

Thorfinn looked very surprised. 'I will not become

your thrall, if that is what you have in mind, Icelander. I prefer death to slavery. So would you.'

'I said you are to have full rights. You are a free man. You may keep your faith and all your property.' Kari glanced at Elf for a moment, and then added, 'Except the slave.'

Thorfinn narrowed his eyes. 'I am free to go ashore with the others?'

'If that's what you want. But I am offering you a free passage, Viking. Maybe there is a better fate for you in Iceland. There is plenty of work to be had on the farms.'

Thorfinn looked intently at Kari, then at Elf.

'You give me your word? I remain a free man, and may worship whatever god I choose?'

'I swear it,' Kari replied.

Thorfinn shrugged his shoulders. 'Then it's all the same to me. I go where Thor wills. I've heard they have fine horses in Iceland.' He pulled out his own silver neck-charm and kissed it, as if to thank his god for saving him. At the same time he fixed Elf with a penetrating stare, although there was nothing on his face to show that he was at all grateful to her for saving his life.

Just then Kari caught sight of Olaf who, encouraged by the lull in the noise and confusion, had crept out of his hiding hole.

'You, boy, come here!' Olaf walked forward very timidly, and glanced uneasily at the other members of the crew.

'Nobody will hurt you now,' Kari reassured him. 'What is your name, boy?'

'Olaf, Master.'

'You are from Danemarc?'

'From Shetland, Master. But my father was from Norway. From Hordaland.'

Kari nodded. 'When we get to Iceland I shall take the pair of you to my father and mother. You will help on our farm. My parents will treat you fairly, I can promise you that.'

Olaf stammered, 'A farm . . . I am to work on a farm?'

'We are all farmers in Iceland. Is that not to your liking, boy?'

'Oh yes, Master. Yes it is. Very much.'

Kari turned to Elf. 'And you, little slave,' he said. 'What is your name, child?'

'Aelflida, Master. I'm from Angle land.' She paused, and added hopefully, 'My friends call me Elf.'

Kari smiled again. 'Then I shall call you Elf also. I was right. You have the Luck, little slave. I saw it in your face the moment I set eyes on you. The Luck is considered a great thing among us, few people have it.' He lowered his voice. 'And we certainly have need of it now, for the men think I have offended the god Thor.' He pinched her cheek, then called out to the crew, 'Make sail! We sail north! We sail for Iceland!'

Into the Vikings' Hall

Shortly before midsummer, after three long weeks at sea, they made a landfall on the south coast of Iceland.

The seafarers were eager to be off to their homesteads after an absence of nearly two years. Kari hired some pack ponies and set off, with Elf and Olaf riding one behind the other, for his father's farm. This was about half a day's ride away in the mountains, at a place called Thorolfsfell. Redbeard rode with them, but he did not say much to anyone.

They reached Thorolfsfell farm at mid-evening time. The buildings were so completely covered over with thick green turf that the farmstead appeared to be a part of the hillside. Only thin wisps of smoke, rising from underneath the eaves of the roof, gave the dwellings away.

Kari gave a shout and jumped off his pony. The travellers were surrounded by a throng of welcoming people. One of the men ran off to fetch Kari's father, who was busy at the sheep-shearing. A tall, handsome woman came out of the hall. She had long fair hair streaked with grey, and was wearing an embroidered apron and a woollen shawl.

Elf, weary from travel, watched as the woman embraced Kari, her kind face full of smiles. Suddenly great hot tears welled up in Elf's eyes and a longing to be cradled in warm, comforting arms engulfed her. She had not seen a woman since the day when she had last seen her own mother. She hid her face in Olaf's rough tunic.

Then she was being lifted from the pony's back and set down in the midst of the chattering group. Olaf slid down beside her.

'Slaves,' a girl whispered, pointing at Olaf's iron neck-ring. Elf noticed that none of the girls from the homestead was wearing a slave collar.

'Come,' said the woman who was Kari's mother. 'Come inside and rest.'

It was several minutes before Elf's eyes became accustomed to the gloom inside the building. She wrinkled up her nose. The whale-oil lamps which were used to light the hall gave off an acrid smell, and the smoke from the long hearth made her eyes water. Several girls of about her own age pressed around her, fingering her ragged clothing and staring at her thin face.

Kari's father Sigurd arrived, bursting into the hall with a roar of welcome.

'Kari Sigurdarson! *Welcome*! Welcome home!' he shouted. He flung himself into the high-seat, the great carved-oak chair reserved for the head of the family. 'You look magnificent, my boy!' He leaned back to get a better look at Kari's splendid new clothes. 'Had good raiding? I can see you have! Just like your father and grandfather before you!'

Sigurd was a huge man, with a very red face and a grey beard. Although he was very rich and powerful it amused him to dress like a simple farmer and he always wore a pair of striped breeches tucked into his muddy boots, and a moulting sealskin jerkin.

Serving men now brought foaming horns of ale and distributed them around the hall. Sigurd raised his drinking horn in both hands.

'To the Viking hero returned in triumph!' he called out. Everybody drank deeply.

'*Heill* Kari!' they shouted. '*Heill! Heill! Heill!*'

Kari rose to speak, but at this moment another man entered the hall. He had a dark beard and tightly curling hair, and seemed to wear a permanently sneering expression on his face. 'Welcome home, brother,' this new arrival said, nodding without much warmth to Kari. It was Skamkel, Kari's elder brother. Sigurd did not even turn to greet him, he was so full of the return of his favourite son.

'Come along, my boy!' he roared. 'Let's see your wounds!' Everybody in the hall cheered and banged the pointed ends of their drinking horns on the tables.

Kari cleared his throat. 'I am afraid I have no wounds, Father . . .' The banging on the tables gradually clattered into silence. Sigurd frowned, as if he had misheard.

'*No wounds*?' he repeated. 'Has Odin brought you unscathed through every battle? I cannot believe it . . .'

Skamkel, who had been helping himself to some cheese and ale from the kitchen place, paused for a moment, sensing that there was something odd about his brother's manner. Sigurd himself took a long draught of ale and sat back in the high seat.

'What are you trying to tell me, Kari Sigurdarson? Have you too disgraced me like that other scapegrace son of mine? Well?'

Kari did not reply.

'Then where is your treasure? Where are all the slaves you have taken?'

'I have brought only these two.' Kari indicated Elf and Olaf with his drinking horn. They both cowered behind one of the massive wooden posts which supported the roof.

'*These*?' Sigurd shouted, as he surveyed them with a scornful expression. 'You have been away for *two whole years* and all you have brought back is these, these . . .' Unable to find words to express his contempt, Sigurd reached for his drinking horn and emptied it at a gulp.

Kari raised his voice above the murmuring which had broken out around the hall. 'I do not want them treated as common slaves. They are to be a part of our household. Of our family.'

Sigurd wiped his mouth on his sleeve. 'Well,' he said after a while. 'You must have done *some* successful raiding, even to get two slaves. You still did better than Skamkel here. He ended up a slave himself.'

Skamkel sipped his ale quietly, ignoring the laughter at his expense. Despite his father favouring his younger brother, he was determined to sit in the high-seat one day, even if he had to kill Kari to get there. Then he would do the laughing.

Kari said, 'I did not do any raiding at all, Father. These two I found on a ship which raided us.' There was a ripple of laughter around the hall. 'We defended ourselves.'

Sigurd gave a groan. 'I don't want to hear about it, you milksop! You have shamed and disgraced me! No raiding; no treasure; nothing. You have done no better than your idiot brother! I shall be a laughing stock at the assembly. Lodmund Ulfsson's son Melkolf brought back *forty* slaves, including a *princess*! A King's daughter out of Ireland! And all you bring back is two puling whelps!' He gestured angrily towards Elf and Olaf. 'Take them outside and kill them! I've got no use for them here!'

The children clung tightly to one another. Skamkel, always glad of an opportunity of getting back into favour, hastily swallowed a piece of cheese and strode across towards them. He clicked his fingers. One of the men threw him a sword. Kari rose from his seat, but before he could speak his mother stood up and spoke in a commanding voice.

'Stop!' she cried to Skamkel, who had already grabbed Olaf and Elf and was pushing them towards the doorway.

Skamkel made a sour face but obeyed his mother.

She turned to her husband. 'You have said yourself, Sigurd Asgrimsson, that Asjolf is getting too old to manage the sheep by himself. Well then, let the boy help him. Nobody else seems to want the job. And I shall take the girl. I am short-handed with the weaving as it is.'

Sigurd glared at her for a moment, then leaned down to retrieve his fallen drinking horn. He made an impatient gesture. 'All right, Gunnhild Hallstein's-daughter,' he said, glancing fiercely at the trembling slaves. 'But they'd better prove worth their keep, do you hear? Or I'll sell them in the autumn. You! More ale here!' He tossed his empty drinking horn to one of the serving men, then turned and noticed Thorfinn Redbeard for the first time. He was sitting quietly at the end of one of the tables, sipping ale. 'Who's this, then?' Sigurd growled.

'A guest,' Kari replied. 'Thorfinn Redbeard is seeking work on one of the farms. I thought perhaps . . .'

'I don't need anybody. Let him try Lodmund Ulfsson. Is this all you've brought back, two slaves and a *guest*? Have you forgotten all our ways?'

'I have changed my ways,' said Kari in a quiet clear voice. 'I no longer follow your god, Father. I serve the White *Kristr* . . .'

'The *what*?' Sigurd exploded and Kari's explanations were lost in his father's rantings. He seemed to have forgotten the two slaves.

'Come, you two,' Gunnhild said hurriedly to Elf and Olaf, in case her husband changed his mind. Although her manner was stern and commanding, Sigurd's wife seemed kind. They followed her to the far end of the hall. She sat them on the stone step beside the cooking pit, gave them each a bowl of thick white curds and warmed some milk for them. They could hear Sigurd shouting angrily in the main part of the hall. He was beside himself with fury on account of Kari's change of religion, especially as he himself was a priest of the god Frey, and he expected all his family to honour his own gods.

While they sat and sipped the curds a girl with long, golden hair walked over and looked them up and down.

'Mother, what ugly creatures,' she remarked to Gunnhild. 'Why does my father not have them killed? They are no use to us here.'

Elf glanced up at her. The girl looked only a couple of years older than she was herself, although she was much taller. She was strikingly beautiful, but her lips curled haughtily and she had Sigurd's fierce-looking eyes.

Gunnhild said, 'You are always complaining that you have too much to do, Rannveig. So you should be glad of the extra help.' She stirred the milk in a metal pan, and dropped in a knob of butter.

'I suppose the girl-thing can help me with my dresses, and comb my hair for me. If it *is* a girl. It is so ugly I can't tell.' She peered closely into Elf's face. 'Yes, I suppose it is. Good. I need a slave of my own now.' She tossed her golden hair and strode off.

After a supper of boiled mutton the members of the family retired to their sleeping closets. Sigurd and Kari had carried on arguing the whole evening. Finally Sigurd shouted, 'I'll not have this blasphemous talk at my hearth, do you hear? You'll worship the gods of your forefathers in your father's hall.' With that he strode into his sleeping closet and banged down the wooden partition angrily.

All the farmhands and their families slept where they could on either side of the long hearth in the hall, spreading out goose-down mattresses and woollen blankets on the floor. Elf and Olaf found a spare place at the far end, beside the cooking pit, and they were soon fast asleep. It had been a long and very bewildering day.

Next morning, Elf was given a slave collar. The smith bent Elf's neck over an anvil, and hammered the red hot ends of the collar together. She flinched at each blow, but the man was skilful and did not hurt her. Her neck was protected by a woollen cloth.

The collar felt heavy and strange at first, but there was so much to do, and so many new things to learn, that after a few days she hardly noticed it at all. Most of the other girls were the daughters of freed slaves or hired hands, so that Elf was the only actual slave girl in the household. As a result she was immediately given all the dirtiest and most wearisome tasks, like sweeping out the hearth, and cleaning out the bath house.

The girls spent most of the day standing in the gloomy hall, working at the spinning and weaving, but apart from this there were the cows and ewes to be milked, the clothes to be washed, the fires to be kept alight, water to be carried and floors to be swept. And as if all this were not enough, Sigurd's daughter Rannveig seemed to regard Elf as her own personal house-slave, so that the poor girl never seemed to have a moment's rest.

'Can't you be more careful!' Rannveig screeched at her one afternoon as Elf attempted to comb out the tangles in her precious golden hair. 'And hurry up! I'm expected in the hall.'

That day a big feast was being held at the farm, to celebrate the homecoming of her brother Kari. In

Sigurd's opinion there was precious little to celebrate, but if he failed to give a feast he would lose face among his neighbours. He and Kari were hardly on speaking terms now.

'That's enough!' Rannveig said airily, and hit Elf on the head with the handle of a walrus-bone hairbrush. 'Now fetch my aprons. And you can take that surly expression off your face, you ugly little Celt.'

'I'm not a Celt, I'm an Angle,' Elf retorted defiantly.

'Don't answer me back, you vicious little slave! I don't care what you call yourself, you're all savages where you come from!' Rannveig aimed another blow at her rebellious attendant. 'Come on, don't just stand there! Fetch my aprons!'

All the Icelandic girls wore two of these aprons, one at the back and one at the front, attached by shoulder straps and pinned to their long, pleated smocks with brooches.

'How miserable you must be on account of being so ugly,' Rannveig said spitefully as Elf brought over a pair of blue aprons, embroidered in white. 'Nobody will ever want to marry *you*, you are so perfectly hideous.'

Elf bit her lip, and tried to concentrate on attaching the shoulder straps to Rannveig's aprons. The older girl chattered on, admiring her reflection in a polished metal mirror.

'Halldor Arnulfsson from Hofdabrekka says he will kill anyone else who marries me. He is desperately in love with me, and he is not yet thirteen. But I think I shall break his heart instead. They have such a small farm after all, and only four cows, and it is very far from here so I would not be able to see my father and mother as often as I liked. Besides, he has freckles. I detest freckles. You have freckles, don't you, you ugly little Celt?' She twisted Elf's head around by prodding her nose painfully with the hairbrush. 'On your nose. How *detestably* ugly you are. All Celts have freckles. How I *hate* you. Celt! Celt! Celt!' and she beat Elf gleefully.

Just then Gunnhild's arrival saved Elf from further torments.

'Rannveig!' Gunnhild said sternly. 'You are insulting our guests by your lateness. I will not have it!'

They could hear laughter and shouting coming from the hall, where the feast had already been underway for some time. Rannveig always liked to keep everybody waiting whenever her father had guests, in order to draw more attention to herself when she finally made an entrance.

'It is the slave's fault, Mother,' she whined. 'She is lazy and idle. I shall tell my father to have her whipped.'

'You shall do nothing of the kind. Run along, girl. You are needed to fetch more ale from the store-house.'

'Yes, Mistress,' said Elf meekly.

'Am I to plait my own hair, Mother? It is too much! I shall not do it!'

Elf scuttled off, glad to be saved the painful chore of coping with Rannveig's long hair.

It was a very light evening, and on the way she stopped to talk to the ponies, who were all standing with their backs to the wind in the walled paddock just above the farm.

'Hullo, *bokki*!' Elf called out to her favourite, a little dun coloured stallion with a dark streak along his back.

The little pony came trotting across to the wall, and nuzzled her hand.

'Sorry *bokki*, no food this time. I'll try and slip out later with some. How would that be?' The pony snorted and tossed his head. He was very fond of dried herring, which Elf had sometimes managed to smuggle out of the food store for him. She stroked his rough coat, which was a beautiful sandy-yellow colour.

All the Icelandic ponies were very small, and none of them stood much higher than a man's elbow at the shoulder. But they were a very strong breed, and could carry a fully armed warrior with ease over the roughest country. They had plump bodies and shaggy coats to protect them from the cold, and long untidy manes which hung down over their eyes and gave them all a very cheeky expression. Elf found them all adorable, especially this one, who seemed to be the leader of the herd. His name, she had discovered, was *Freyfaxi*.

A burst of laughter and shouting reminded her that she was needed in the hall.

She looked round at the odd, treeless landscape, so different from everything she was used to. Iceland was a strange and stony place. Even the rich green meadows around the farm were strewn with rocks and boulders, and they soon gave way to barren crags of twisted black rock. Across the valley, the ice mountains shone with a dull gleam in the evening sunlight. The sight of the silent white peaks always frightened her, and she could easily believe the tales she had heard of the trolls and frost giants who were supposed to live in the ice.

She sighed. This bleak-looking country was her home now, and probably always would be. The marshlands and creeks of the land of her birth were already a faded memory.

'Goodbye, *bokki*,' she whispered to the pony, and hurried off to fetch the ale.

Among the Horse Eaters

Elf staggered into the hall, tottering a little under the weight of the ale. Smoke rose from the fire; the oil lamps gave a dim light and the noise of revelry was deafening. Her eyes wandered around the hall. Tables had been set out on either side of the hearth, down the whole length of the hall. All the guests were packed together on the benches, laughing, shouting, singing and sipping ale from drinking horns. All sorts of delicacies had already been served, including sheep's heads, roast puffin, and boiled goose. Everybody was in a very merry mood.

Kari was at his place next to Sigurd, and Skamkel sat on the other side of his father. Elf looked for Thorfinn Redbeard, and saw him at last at the bottom of a table among some visiting farmers.

Rannveig had taken her place on the raised platform at the far end of the hall, which was reserved for the female members of the family and the wives of the more important guests. She drew many admiring glances from the young men – and jealous ones from the girls.

'Boy! More ale!' Sigurd bellowed.

Olaf, who was acting as serving-boy for the occasion, hurried to refill Sigurd's drinking horn from one of the large vessels at the side of the hall. He had quite lost his pinched, frightened look, and his cheeks now glowed from the many hours he spent in the keen air of Thorolfsfell. Elf had seen very little of him during their first week, for he had been very busy helping with the sheep-shearing. Now she caught his eye, and they smiled at each other across the smokey hall.

Sigurd rose unsteadily to his feet.

'All-high!' he bellowed at the top of his voice, raising his drinking horn towards the roof of the hall. 'Battle father! Spear-thruster! *Grimnir! Gondlir! Svidrir! Odin!*'

'Odin!' all the guests repeated, rising to their feet, and holding out their drinking horns in front of them. Following Sigurd, they drank in honour of the god. Kari raised his horn to his lips, but took none of the ale. Sigurd did not notice.

As she moved down the hall replenishing drinking vessels, Elf glanced uneasily at the swords, axes and shields which hung on the wall, momentoes of Sigurd's Viking days. In one corner stood a huge broad-bladed axe called 'troll-cleaver'. She had heard it said that Sigurd had killed a troll with it, inside a burial mound in Norway.

Sigurd was now reciting the names of the god Thor. His voice rang around the hall.

'Mighty one! Hammerer! Thunderer! Chariot-rider! Son-of-Odin! *Thor*!'

'*Thor*!' echoed the guests, raising their drinking horns. Again Kari did not drink, and again Sigurd did not notice. Then, in the silence which followed, a sneering voice was heard from the centre of the hall.

'*My brother does not drink . . .*'

Skamkel was holding out his drinking horn and pointing accusingly at Kari. His face wore its habitually sour-looking expression.

'Is our humble ale not to your taste, brother?' he enquired acidly. 'Or is it the gods you wish to insult?'

Kari did not reply. He knew that Skamkel was deliberately provoking a quarrel.

All eyes turned towards Kari.

'Drink, Kari Sigurdarson!' Sigurd roared, turning on him. 'Drink, curse you! I'll not have the gods dishonoured by a son of mine!'

'It is forbidden to me to drink to other gods,' said Kari, in his still, clear voice.

'You'll worship the gods of your fore-fathers in my hall, boy! Do you hear me? I'll have none of this blasphemous talk here!'

Skamkel, who was standing on the other side of his father, smirked with satisfaction. Things were turning out just as he had hoped.

Sigurd glared at Kari and carried on with the ceremony.

'Lord of stallions!' he called out. 'All beautiful! Green one! Bringer-of-the-dew! Glory-of-elves! *Frey*!'

'*Frey*!' everybody repeated, drinking to the third god. Serving girls ran down the hall serving meat. By chance it fell to Elf to serve Kari, and she was trembling as she placed the wooden dish on the table in front of him. He did not look round at her, but continued to stare fixedly at Skamkel, who was eyeing him with a twisted smile.

Sigurd now held up his dish and recited the traditional midsummer prayer to the god of the earth:

'Lord Frey, hear us!
In your hall, brighter-than-sunlight
Accept our sacrifice.
From the ash tree, Yggdrasil
Scatter your dew
Upon the earth!'

Everybody then sat down and began to eat. Everybody except Kari. Then Skamkel's voice once more echoed around the hall.

'*My brother does not eat . . .*'

Elf caught her breath.

Sigurd lurched to his feet in a blind fury and stabbed a forefinger at Kari. 'You will eat, do you hear? You insult the god Frey at his feast! You will eat the flesh of the sacred horse. I command you to eat!'

'I will not, Father. My God forbids it.'

'Your God! The god of milksops! The god of trembling, whey-face cowards!'

He staggered from the table and picked up the great axe 'troll-cleaver' from its corner. 'Get out, you sickly whelp!' he raged, raising the axe into the air. 'You're no longer a son of mine! Do you hear me? If you ever show your face here again, I swear I'll kill you!'

An ugly sneer of triumph spread across Skamkel's face.

Kari looked calmly round the hall, then stood up and slowly walked towards the door. He nodded for Olaf to bring his riding cloak and then, with a last look at his father, opened the door and walked out.

A chill wind gusted in through the open doorway and made the whale-oil lamps flicker wildly. No one uttered a word.

'Curse you!' roared Sigurd and hurled the axe after the retreating figure. The blade smashed into the door post and held fast.

Wrapping his cloak around him Kari strode across the yard to the paddock to collect his ponies. It was late, but still quite light; the strange, bright twilight of the far northern summer. As he slipped a halter on to the freshest of his ponies, he heard a noise behind him, and turned.

'Hello, Elf,' he said, surprised. 'What are you doing out here?'

'I slipped out of the back. Take me with you, *Aetheling* . . .'

'I have to go and beg a place to sleep in front of somebody else's hearth, Elf. I cannot take you with me.'

'Can't I be your slave, *Aetheling*?'

'No, I'm sorry Elf, but I'm going to Kirkubyr. It's a Christian settlement and I won't have a household there of my own.' He slung his pack bags over the pony's back.

Elf looked very sad and desolate. At that moment the little dun-coloured pony, hearing her voice, came trotting over to them.

'Hello, *bokki*,' she said, stroking his muzzle. She turned to Kari. 'He's my favourite.'

'This pony! I shouldn't get too fond of him if I were you, Elf. He's a sacred horse.'

'Sacred?'

'To the god Frey. That's why he's called Freyfaxi. Didn't you know?' Elf shook her head.

'What does it mean,' Elf asked, continuing to stroke the pony, 'if he's sacred?'

'It means no one may ride him. It means . . .' Kari hesitated, not wanting to upset her. 'That meat at my father's feast . . . it was sacred meat. Meat from a horse they sacrificed this morning. *He* was a sacred horse. You understand?'

Elf nodded. Slowly the truth dawned on her. The cheeky little pony with the untidy mane was going to be sacrificed to Sigurd's cruel god. And then, they would *eat* him . . . at a feast . . . just like tonight. '*You will eat the flesh of the sacred horse*,' Kari's father had said.

'When?' she whispered, horrified.

'I don't know. Next Yule, or midsummer next year. I'm sorry, Elf. People like my father will never give up the old ways.'

'May I not even stroke him?' Kari shook his head again. 'Come away from him, Elf,' he said gently. 'It's better to have nothing to do with him.' He pulled her away from the wall of the paddock. Freyfaxi leaned his neck over, trying to reach her, nibbling the edge of her pinafore trying to find her pockets.

Elf felt that her heart would break. How could they think of killing such a cheerful, affectionate animal? She bit her lip. She would never understand the Norsemen and their cruel ways. Never!

Kari saw her distress and put an arm around her shoulder. 'Come. Cheer up, Elf. Soon you will be going to the summer farm. There are plenty of other ponies. You will be able to learn to ride while you're up there, I'm sure of it.'

'The summer farm?' Elf repeated, swallowing back her tears.

'Nobody has told you about the summer farm? We send all the animals up into the mountains every summer for the grass. We have a small farm in a valley called Godaland. Up there, you see, towards the glaciers. You are sure to be sent there, all the girls go every year to look after the dairy.'

Elf brightened. 'Shall I really go too?'

'I'm sure of it. There is not much to do at the home farm, not once the animals have gone. You will live up there for the whole of the summer. It's a wonderful place. I used to go up there every year when I was a boy.'

'But I shall miss you, *Aetheling*. Will you never come back?'

'That depends on my father. But I shall come and visit you in Godaland before you come down for the winter. How would that be?'

'You promise?'

'I promise. And you must promise me that you will never go near that pony.' He could see her glancing wistfully towards the paddock. 'Any of the others, but not that one, understand. I don't want any harm to come to you, now that I won't be here to protect you.'

'Harm? What harm?'

'My father will have sworn an oath to kill anybody who rides that pony. That always happens when a horse is given to the god. And he'd do it too. Our people cannot break an oath once they have sworn it.'

Kari lightly touched his hand to her forehead. 'Goodbye, Elf,' he said. 'Give me some of your luck for I shall need it more than ever now.'

Elf watched him as he mounted his horse and rode down towards the river, with two spare ponies trotting behind. Just before he went out of sight around the side of an overhanging crag, he waved. Then he was gone.

Summer Farm

A few days later preparations began for the move to the summer farm. The girls busied themselves packing blankets, rugs, cooking utensils, cheese presses; all the things that would be needed were packed into saddle-bags, ready for loading on to the pack ponies on the morning of their departure. Elf was to go to help with the milking and the cheese making, but she learned with relief that Rannveig, Sigurd's spiteful daughter was not going with them.

At last the day came, and after a hearty breakfast of curds and cold mutton they all said goodbye to the home farm until the autumn, and set off for the mountains.

The ponies pranced along happily in front, about twenty or thirty of them, with Freyfaxi leading the way, snorting proudly and tossing his mane. Several of the mares had foals running beside them and more would be born up at the lush pasture. Sigurd and several of the men rode beside them. Then came the great bleating mass of sheep with Asjolf the shepherd, and Olaf the apprentice shepherd, walking behind with sticks. Next were the four cows, with all the girls guiding them from behind. Elf had a very long stick, and was driving a big brown cow called Audumla. And last of all came the long line of pack ponies, all roped together, with a great jingle-jangle load of pots and pans and other baggage strung on to their backs.

Everyone was happy and there was singing and laughter as the band wound along the paths up into the mountains.

They had to wade through several icy torrents before starting the final climb. The ponies loved the water, but some of the sheep were reluctant to cross and had to be hauled over. Luckily even the freezing water failed to dampen everybody's high spirits.

After passing through a narrow, stony pass, they seemed to emerge quite suddenly into the high valley country of Godaland. As they came round the corner of a rocky crag, Elf had to shade her eyes. They were almost completely surrounded now by the dazzling glaciers which caught the sunshine and bathed the dales in their reflected light. The valley in front of them was covered by great expanses of lush green grass, and coppices of dwarf birch trees clung to the steep slopes. These were the first trees that Elf had seen in Iceland.

Everywhere streams raced down from the heights, glinting and sparkling in the light from the glaciers, and rainbows danced above the waterfalls which cascaded down from the ice-cliffs. It was a brighter, lighter, greener, more dazzling place than Elf had ever imagined could exist. Gunnhild had told her that the place was called Godaland because it was said to resemble Ásgard, the dwelling place of the gods. Now she saw why.

The ponies, neighing with excitement, raced away across the slopes, wheeling madly about and kicking their hooves up in delight. The sheep poured eagerly over the green turf and immediately fell to cropping the lush grass.

Soon they came to the summer farm itself. There were two buildings, a living-house and a dairy, together with some open sheepfolds made out of rough stone. The living-house was newly covered in fresh green turf and was lined inside with sweet smelling oak and pine, timber that Sigurd had shipped over specially from Norway as these trees did not exist in Iceland. Everybody flung themselves down on the soft turf and the girls handed round a meal of dried fish and butter.

Sigurd and the other men were returning to the lower farm for the haymaking and, just as soon as their ponies had been rested and fed, they planned to leave. Before departing, Sigurd had a quick word with Asjolf the shepherd and his apprentice.

'You, boy,' he said to Olaf. 'I'm pleased with you. You make sure to learn everything you can while you're up here, I want to train you up as my head shepherd.' Olaf blushed, and adjusted his woollen cap. Sigurd turned to Asjolf. 'See that you teach him to ride properly. You can ride any of the horses boy, except my dun stallion, Freyfaxi. There he is, down there, leading the herd. That animal is a sacred horse, anybody who rides him buys their death at my hands. You understand that?'

'Yes master.'

'Good.' Sigurd hauled himself up into his saddle. 'You will all do as Asjolf and his wife Unn direct you!' he called out. 'They are in charge at the summer farm. I shall come up from time to time to see how you are getting on.'

'Yes master . . .' everybody said.

Sigurd wheeled his pony round and set off at a brisk trot with his men.

Unn immediately instructed the girls to set to work, bringing out all the bedding into the air, sweeping all the floors in the farmhouse, and scrubbing all the tables and shelves in the dairy clean of the dust and grime of winter. They all set about their tasks with a carefree air and sang as they worked, for Sun-month was come and they were at the summer farm at last! Asjolf took Olaf with him to the sheepfold to sort the ewes into separate pens. The male sheep and the young females without lambs would be allowed to wander where they liked over the mountains, but the ewes had to be kept close at hand for milking. It would be Olaf's task to see that the ewes did not wander too far away during the daytime, when they were turned out into the pastures to graze.

After the work was done there was such excitement and such gossipings and gigglings and the evening was so light and bright that nobody thought of sleeping until well towards midnight. Some of the girls went up to the big waterfall behind the farm and climbed right behind the cascade of water. Elf and Olaf went down to the river and spent a long time trying to catch salmon in the rock pools, but without success. Then they too went up to look at the waterfall, and stayed there until the sun finally dipped behind the mountains to the north. It never seemed to get properly dark in Iceland at this time of year.

'Come in! Come in!' They heard Unn calling them, banging a saucepan with her fist. 'Come in or the trolls will get you! Don't think you're safe just because it's summer,' she said, fussing around. 'When the sun goes down, that's when they come out. Have you never heard of the Godaland trolls? See, there, up where the glaciers meet, that's where they'll come down. Won't take them very long to get here either, on their great thick legs. Hurry inside!'

Elf glanced up uneasily at the glaciers. The ice-mountains were bathed in an eerie blue-grey light. Below them, the crags and cliffs were deep in shadow, a darkness that could hide all manner of monsters.

As soon as all the girls were safely inside, old Unn walked up and down in front of the doorway, waving a piece of smoking charcoal in the air, and reciting an incantation against the mountain giants.

'Troll daughter, Fell Walker,
Stay away, Stay away.
Orgelmir, Bergelmir,
Touch us not, touch us not.
Grid, Galp, Geirroth,
Greyback and Graffoloth,
Begone! Begone! Begone!'

As she closed the door, she pointed out a line of four strangely shaped rocks, silhouetted against one of the overhanging tongues of ice and protruding from the glaciers like giant's fingers. 'That's four children who stayed out too late in the time of old Asgrim,' she muttered darkly, without any further explanation.

Elf lay awake for some time thinking of the trolls and the giants up in the glaciers. She imagined them swooping down and snatching her up in great hairy arms. Then she saw the light of burning villages and smelled the smoke. She sat bolt upright. But it was only the smoke from the hearth and the light of an Icelandic summer night which troubled her sleep. She tried to remember her old home in Angle land but the images were fading.

At last she slept – but not for long.

She started and sat up. She could hear harsh, wheezing breaths, accompanied by a strange scraping noise. A piece of turf dislodged itself from the roof and earth showered on to her face.

'Olaf! Olaf! Wake up!' She shook him. He turned over and opened his eyes sleepily.

'What . . .?' he murmured.

'There's trolls on the roof,' Elf hissed. 'Listen . . .'

Baa! *Baa*!

Olaf shook Elf, laughing. 'It's not trolls, stupid. It's sheep! It's sheep eating the grass on the roof. I'd better go and chase them off.'

'You're not going out there,' she squeaked. 'Not on your own.'

'Come with me then.'

None of the others was awake as they crept silently from their sleeping places and out into the fresh, bright air. The sun was already up, somewhere behind the mountains. It was still invisible from where they were standing, but they could see the white glow in the sky. Most of the valley was still bathed in shadows, but the great glaciers were shining in the dawn, sending a strange wash of reflected light over the whole of Godaland. The world seemed to have turned grey and silver, and all the colours of daylight hours were missing.

'Shoo, shoo, you dreadful trolls,' cried Olaf.

Elf laughed and sat on the top of the roof beside her friend. For the first time since they had known each other, there was nobody to tell them what to do or what not to do.

Olaf's favourite sheepdog, Frekki, came to the end of his chain, and Olaf went down to stroke him.

'Hello, Frekki . . .' Olaf said, patting the dog, a happy looking Viking collie with a pointed muzzle, a brown coat and a beautiful white chest.

As she stroked the dog Elf looked up. A blaze of

copper-gold light had suddenly flashed on to the top of the big glacier, as the invisible sun rose higher in the north-eastern sky. It was such a majestic sight that Elf thought somebody really ought to be blowing a great horn to greet the dawn. When she looked round, Olaf had gone.

'Elf, come here!' He was standing at the top of the grassy rise at the back of the farm. 'Look,' he said, as she caught up with him. 'It's that pony. The one we mustn't ride.'

Freyfaxi the sacred pony was standing a short distance away, beside a group of large rocks. His long, shaggy mane, which hung over his forehead as usual, was lit up by the reflected sunbeams from the glacier, while the rest of his body was still in shadow. The strange, silvery light seemed to transform the plump little animal into quite another sort of being, and for once Freyfaxi really did look sacred, some creature of the air and mountains, without substance.

'He's been standing there watching us all the time,' Olaf said, uneasily. He leaned down and let the sheepdog off the chain.

As soon as Freyfaxi was quite sure that they had seen him he gave a soft snort and trotted a few paces away, swishing his tail. Then he stopped, and turned his head to look at them.

Elf gripped Olaf's arm. '*He's asking us to go with him,*' she whispered. She had no idea why she was whispering. No one was about.

Olaf frowned. 'We can't. We're supposed to be asleep . . .'

'Frightened of trolls?' Elf grinned impishly.

'Of course I'm not.'

'Come on then.' She tugged his sleeve, and Olaf reluctantly followed as Elf ran over to the waiting pony.

'Hello, *bokki*,' she said, putting her arms around the pony's neck. Freyfaxi nuzzled her shoulder, then, with a snort, bounded off across the rocky ground. Elf and Olaf looked at each other for a moment, and then followed, finding it difficult to keep up with the sure-footed pony as he led the way across rocky stream beds, through the sparse woods of dwarf birch, then along the riverbank towards the head of the valley and the glaciers. Frekki the sheepdog bounded along happily at their heels.

Freyfaxi reached the top of the knoll, looked back for a moment to make sure that they were following, then disappeared over the crest of the ridge.

They followed, breathless from the long walk. At the top they halted. The end of the valley formed a great bowl-shaped pasture of soft grass, which lay cradled beneath the silent and gleaming ice-mountains. Just below them all the ponies were racing around the pasture in a wide circle, tossing their heads and neighing, as if in some wild midsummer horse-dance. Freyfaxi was standing a little way down the slope, looking back at them.

The two friends walked quickly down the slope. As they approached, the ponies drew back to let them through, and in a moment they found themselves in the centre of this enchanted circle of tossing manes and gleaming eyes. Slowly, the ponies came to a halt, blowing and snorting, then stood jostling each other as Freyfaxi pushed his way through to the centre of the circle. He walked up to Elf, and lowered his head in front of her.

She took hold of his mane. 'He wants me to ride him,' she whispered. 'I know he does. He's asking me.'

Olaf swung round. 'You can't!' he cried out. 'Not that one. He's sacred. Sigurd said . . .'

'Sigurd?' Elf said in a strange voice. She hopped on to a hummock of turf. Freyfaxi moved over beside her. One tiny jump and she would be sitting on his back.

'Don't, Elf! Please don't! He belongs to Sigurd!'

'No he doesn't. Do you *bokki*? Not really. He doesn't belong to anybody. And neither,' she added defiantly, 'do we. Besides, Sigurd's not here, so he'll never know.'

Once again the sunlight flashed from the face of the glacier. Olaf looked pleadingly at his companion, but she only grinned back at him. She looked more than ever like some mischievous light-elf sprung from the mountains. Next moment she was sitting on the pony's back.

'Elf! Get off! Get off! He'll kill you! Sigurd will kill you if he finds out! You heard what he said!' But even as Olaf pleaded he felt the thrill of what she had done. She had defied their master. That meant that underneath they were still free, they were not really slaves.

'I'm *riding*!' Elf yelled delightedly. 'Look Olaf, I'm riding!' The pony walked forward, then slowly broke into a bouncing trot.

Then, feeling that she was gaining in confidence, the pony began lifting his legs one at a time in a circular motion, adopting the high, prancing gait peculiar to the Icelandic ponies.

Elf found that the motion of the *tolt* was much smoother than the bumping trot with which Freyfaxi had started the lesson. Although Freyfaxi himself was bouncing his hooves on the smooth turf, his body moved along quite evenly, and Elf began to think that there was nothing to riding after all, and that she could go on like this for hours.

'Faster, *bokki*,' she said, patting his neck. Freyfaxi lifted his hooves even higher, and swished his tail proudly.

‘Look Olaf!’ Elf called out. ‘I can ride! I can really ride!’ Forgetting in her excitement to grip properly with her knees, she turned and waved to Olaf, and almost immediately flew backwards over the pony’s tail, landing with a bump on the grass. Fortunately the turf was soft and bouncy, so that she came to no harm.

‘Are you all right?’ Olaf shouted, catching up with her. Freyfaxi walked back and began to nuzzle Elf’s face, snorting softly as if he was trying to tell her where she had gone wrong.

‘I’m all right,’ Elf said, sitting up and smiling. ‘It was wonderful, Olaf.’

Olaf looked very doubtful. ‘You’ve done it now,’ he said seriously. ‘If the master ever finds out . . .’

‘He won’t. Come on. Try riding one of the other ponies. He said that would be all right, didn’t he?’

A chestnut pony with a white star on his forehead had stopped just behind Freyfaxi. He had a long, golden mane, and seemed fairly docile. Olaf decided to try riding him. He looked awkward but managed to climb on to the pony’s back. Elf took a running leap and swung herself up on to her own mount.

‘Ready?’ she called out. Olaf, looking rather frightened, gripped on tightly and nodded. ‘Go on, *bokki*,’ Elf said. ‘Off you go.’ Freyfaxi moved off smoothly, and was soon lifting his hooves in the prancing rhythm of the *tolt*, while Olaf’s pony obediently followed behind him. This time Elf remembered to grip with her knees as she rode, and soon found that she could do this almost without thinking. Olaf was less successful, and now discovered that riding was more difficult than it looked. After kicking rather too heftily with his heels in an effort to catch up with Elf, he suddenly found himself lying on his back in a patch of boggy ground while his pony trotted calmly on.

'It must be easier when you know how,' he muttered, getting to his feet. His breeches felt wet and muddy, but apart from that he was unhurt, and he was determined not to be defeated by the pony which had stopped a little distance away and, Olaf could have sworn, was actually *laughing* at him.

He scrambled on to the pony's back again and this time was much more successful. He found that once he got the animal into a *tolt* pace it was far less bumpy and much easier to sit upright.

After a few more circles Olaf felt much more confident. Now they were both really riding! Faster and faster they went, until Freyfaxi, letting out a whinny of delight, changed his gait to a much faster pace, keeping his legs straight and bouncing madly across the grass. Elf clung on tightly to his mane, half afraid now that they were going so fast, but shrieking with triumph at the same time. Freyfaxi swung round, leading his herd in a wild circuit of the pastures. All the ponies followed their leader, pounding their hooves on the turf, jostling each other, and wheeling round in an ever tightening circle. Both their faces were shining, their cheeks rosy with the exhilaration of their first gallop. They finally came to a halt in the centre of the pasture, and gazed around them breathlessly.

'Look!' Elf cried. 'What's that?' Over on the far side of the valley, beneath the dark crags, they could see strange jets of silvery vapour rising out of the shadows towards the sunlight. 'It looks like smoke, or steam. Let's go and have a look.'

Olaf looked rather sheepish. 'I don't know if I can

make this pony go where I want,' he admitted. 'I've just been sitting tight and following you.'

'I'll go first then. Come on *bokki*.' Elf patted Freyfaxi's neck, and he obediently trotted off in the direction of the strange-looking clouds of steam. Olaf's pony followed.

They soon reached the rocky ground at the edge of the mountain, where sheer cliffs rose up towards the tongues of ice far above. Steam was hissing out of a cleft in the splintered black rock, and they could see clouds of vapour rising from a stream which gushed out of the base of the cliffs. Some rocks and mossy pieces of turf had piled themselves across the path of the stream, forming a natural dam. The stream flowed into a hollow, forming a large pool of steaming water.

Elf jumped down, and ran to the edge of the water. 'It's hot!' she exclaimed delightedly.

'Be careful,' Olaf warned, as he swung himself gingerly down from his pony's back. 'It might be boiling.'

But Elf had already kicked off her boots, and was wading in. She flung off all her clothes and threw them on the moss-covered rocks. The air felt suddenly cold, so she bobbed down into the pool so that the water came up to her shoulders.

'It's wonderful!' she yelled. 'It's lovely and warm! Come on in!'

Olaf pulled off his clothes too, hopped over the rocks, and lowered himself into the pool. The water was deliciously warm.

'Wonderful! Wonderful!' Elf exclaimed again, and ducked her head under the water.

'I wonder what makes it hot?' Olaf said. 'There must be a reason for it.'

'Unn says there are giants living inside the mountain,' Elf suggested. 'Perhaps they've got a fire in there.'

Olaf shook his head. 'I don't believe in giants. There's a strange smell too.' Elf wrinkled up her nose, and nodded, then shrugged her shoulders.

'I don't know what causes it all,' she said. 'But it doesn't matter, does it? It's here, it's beautiful and we found it,' and she splashed joyously.

At last they came out of the pool, glowing and warm. They picked their way across the rocks towards the great expanse of grass, where the ponies were grazing contentedly. Here they turned cartwheels and somersaults, and ran and jumped and danced and shrieked and yelled, with Frekki the sheepdog barking at their heels, and the two ponies bounding along beside. Then Freyfaxi and the chestnut had a good roll on the soft turf, kicking their legs in the air in sheer pleasure.

Elf and Olaf flung themselves exhausted on to the soft grass and watched the sun rise between two distant peaks, and throw its flaming orange light across the valley.

'We'd better go back,' Olaf said. 'Everybody else will be up soon, and we'll be missed.'

Footsteps of the Frost-giants

From that time Elf and Olaf often crept out before any of the others were awake, to ride the ponies and to enjoy the beautiful Icelandic dawn.

The good weather continued for nearly a fortnight, and with it the happy, carefree mood of everybody up at the summer farm. Sigurd was away at the annual Icelandic Assembly, and Asjolf the shepherd was very easy-going with his charges.

'You work hard and please the master,' he would say to Olaf, 'like as not he'll make you the chief shepherd one day and you'll end up earning your freedom. Just like I earned mine from his father, old Asgrim. I get paid now for what I do, see. Twelve elbow-lengths of cloth a year, and my keep. All you've got to do is make sure we don't lose any of his sheep. No worry about feeding or watering 'em, not up here. The gods do that for us.'

One morning Olaf asked the old man, 'What happens if we do lose any, Asjolf?'

'Lose one, the master'll frown, but not say much. Lose two, well, he'll shout at us, and storm a bit. Lose three, you'd better watch out. Lose the lot . . .'

'Yes . . .?'

'Well, boy, you see that crag up there by the glaciers? If we were ever to lose the lot, the pair of us had better climb up there and jump off, I'd reckon. Hey – don't look so frightened, boy! All you have to do is keep your ears open. And if you hear one of them bleating, all piteous and forlorn, more than likely it's stuck down a gulley somewhere on the fells.' The old shepherd explained how easy it was to haul a sheep up the face of a cliff with the help of one of the ponies. 'So never go anywhere without your rope, see? And get one of the ponies that you can trust. They're better than dogs in this sort of country.'

They drove the bleating ewes into the sheepfold where the girls were waiting, ready to start the milking. Elf caught sight of Olaf and waved. Asjolf smiled and nodded.

'My wife Unn, she was one of the dairy-girls here when I first came.' Olaf's mouth dropped open. It was difficult to imagine old Unn ever being young. 'How many ewes have we got, boy?' Asjolf asked him suddenly. 'No looking.'

'Twenty-eight, Asjolf.'

'Good boy. Unless they get stuck down a cliff, you can leave the sheep to look after themselves, but the ewes, *we* have to look after them. Count 'em as they come in for milking, and count 'em into the sheepfold every night. If it helps, give 'em names. That's what I do.'

So life went on at the summer farm, day after happy day. Olaf was soon an accomplished rider – to Asjolf's surprise.

'Well, I've never seen the like,' he remarked one day. 'You must have done some riding before this, whatever you say, boy, to have picked it up so quickly.' Elf and Olaf glanced at one another but said nothing.

Then, quite suddenly, the weather changed and a strong south-east wind drove rain-clouds in from the sea. One drizzly morning, Sigurd arrived from Thorolfsfell on a visit, together with some of his men. Rannveig had come along with them for the ride. Sigurd dismounted beside the sheepfold and ordered Olaf to hobble the horses while he went off on a tour of inspection with Asjolf.

It was a damp, dismal day, and the glaciers above the farm, which in the sunshine had looked so dazzling and majestic, now seemed merely grey, dirty and threatening.

Rannveig, who had remained in her saddle surveying everything with a regal air, now demanded that Olaf fetch a stool from the farmhouse so that she could dismount in comfort.

'And give my horse a good rubbing down too, slave-boy,' she commanded, tossing back the hood of her riding cloak as she stepped down from the pony.

'See you brush her properly under the saddle,' she now said, smiling at him. Olaf scowled, and carried on rubbing down the pony.

'You know,' Rannveig persisted, 'if you did not always have such a disagreeable expression on your face you would be quite a handsome boy.'

Olaf's hand stopped. He closed his eyes for a moment, then carried on brushing the pony's coat with jerking movements. He was quite used to being baited by members of a master's family, having endured all sorts of insults in the shoemaker's workshop in Ireland. He knew instinctively that whatever sweet words were issuing from Rannveig's dainty lips, in her heart she meant to hurt him. He was a slave and she was his master's daughter, nothing could change that.

Rannveig stepped closer to him and ran her fingers through her long, golden hair. 'And where is that slave girl to brush my hair?' she commanded, trying to make Olaf look at her.

Olaf, who was rubbing down one of the pony's back

legs, lifted up the hoof to check for stones, then stood up and faced her. Rannveig, certain that she was about to receive a declaration of love, fluttered her eyelids and gave him one of her most winning smiles.

'Most people say I have quite the most beautiful hair in Iceland,' she lowered her voice and fluttered her eyelids again. 'What do you say, boy?'

Olaf clenched and unclenched his hands over the horse-rag. 'I don't think you've got beautiful hair at all. I think it looks like last year's hay.' Almost immediately he regretted his bold reply.

'How dare you talk to me like that!' Rannveig screeched, her radiant smile changing into an ill-tempered snarl. 'How *dare* you!'

She flew at him, clawing at his face with her fingernails. Olaf, having no doubt that Rannveig would scratch his eyes out if she could, shielded his face with his hands, and tried to push her away. Both of them fell to the ground, rolling in the oozing black mud around the pony's feet.

Rannveig, screeching and yelling, tore an ugly gash in Olaf's cheek. Olaf got hold of her wrists, but she slipped free and leapt at him again. He pushed her back, and managed to force her head down into the mud. At that moment, Sigurd came round the corner of the sheepfold.

Seeing him, Rannveig began yelling even louder. 'Help! Help! Father! Help! He's attacking me! Help!' Sigurd ran towards them, and pulled Olaf to his feet. His face was black as thunder.

'He just set on me, father,' Rannveig wailed. 'Without warning.' She began sobbing. 'I was so frightened. And look at my clothes . . .' Both she and Olaf were covered from head to foot in mud and filth.

Olaf opened his mouth to speak, but before he could

say anything Sigurd caught him a savage blow across the cheek. He flew backwards under the ponies' hooves into the oozing mud.

'Do you dare to lay hands on your master's daughter, slave-boy!' Sigurd bellowed. 'Think yourself lucky I do not kill you on the spot!'

Olaf stood up, trying not to cry. He said nothing. He knew there was no point. Inside, he felt empty and bitter again, just as he had at the shoemaker's.

All the girls had gathered round and were watching in silence. It had begun to drizzle again. Then, in the far distance, they heard a long, deep rumbling sound, like thunder, rolling across the glaciers.

'You should kill him, Father,' Rannveig hissed viciously. 'You see how dangerous he is. If you don't kill him now, he will murder all of us when he is older, you will see.'

Sigurd however seemed to have recovered his temper. 'Get up, boy,' he said coldly. 'I need Asjolf to help with the start of the hay-making. That means you'll have to look after the sheep by yourself for a few days. So make sure you do it properly and don't lose any, do you hear me? I'm watching you, boy. I'm watching you . . .'

That evening, after the ewes had been penned up for the night, Elf found Olaf sitting in the sheepfold with Frekki the sheepdog at his feet. It was still raining, and the water dripped down channels in the rough stone. Olaf's toggle-cloak was soaked through, but he made no effort to move.

'She told him I attacked her,' he said mournfully, as Elf came to sit on a mossy boulder beside him. 'She started it.' He felt his cheek, which still bore the mark of Rannveig's nails.

'She's like that with everybody,' Elf said.

'I'll never become the shepherd now. I'll be a slave for the rest of my life. I wish I'd never come here. I wish they'd killed me along with the shoemaker.'

'I'm sure Sigurd will forget about it. I heard Asjolf telling him what a good shepherd-boy you were becoming.'

'It's just not fair, Elf. I've worked so hard. And he hit me. He hit me really hard, just like the shoemaker did.' He was crying now. Elf took his arm.

'Things aren't so bad really,' she said. 'We can't expect too much, you said so yourself. We're only slaves. But we're still alive. And we're still together, aren't we? We might have been sold to different masters. So we're lucky really.'

'I suppose so.'

'Come on,' Elf said. 'Come inside and have supper.'

After they had eaten, everybody sat around the hearth feeling very dismal and downhearted. Sigurd's visit and the change in the weather, had brought the happy mood of the previous weeks to an end.

They were glad of the fire's crackling warmth. They listened to the hailstones drumming on the turf roof above them. When the hail stopped, it began to sleet. Two of the girls started playing a board game, but they soon gave up and stared gloomily into the fire like the others. Every so often water trickled through gaps in the turf roof and fell hissing into the hearth.

Then Frekki the sheepdog, who had been lying beside the cooking pit, suddenly pricked up his ears and began barking.

'What is it, *bokki*?' Olaf said.

Then they all heard it. A great, deep, distant rumbling

noise. The same noise that they had heard during the afternoon. Then, they had thought it was thunder.

Nobody said a word. The noise started again. What was it? It seemed too harsh to be thunder, somehow. Thunder started with a crash and then rolled away to nothing, while this noise went on and on, like . . .

Like what?

Suddenly they felt the ground tremble. All the girls screamed and clung to each other. Showers of earth cascaded down from the roof.

'*They're coming*!' Unn shrieked. '*The giants are coming*! I can feel their footsteps. They're coming down from the glaciers! Odin protect us, it's the end of the world!'

Quite suddenly, the shaking stopped. 'The prophecy! The prophecy!' Unn continued to shriek. 'The giants are coming! Jormungand is coming! Surt the fire giant is coming!'

'Elf!' Olaf called from the doorway. 'Come here!'

Elf went to the entrance, really trembling now, for it was difficult not to believe in Unn's ravings.

'Look,' Olaf said, pointing outside. The rain and the sleet had stopped, and it now seemed to be snowing. But the snow was *black*.

'Don't go out there!' Elf said urgently, but it was too late. Frowning, Olaf caught one of the black snowflakes in his hand, and poked it with his finger. It left dark smudges on his palm and forefinger.

Elf clutched her cheeks. 'Oh Olaf, what is it? It's the end of the world, isn't it?' Olaf shook his head.

'It's not snow, it's *ash*,' he said, puzzled. He tasted a little of it. 'Ugh!' He spat it out. 'Ash, cinders. But where from?'

Elf whispered, 'Surt, the fire giant . . .' Then they heard the noise again.

'It's not trolls, Elf. Don't be stupid. There must be a reason for it. There's a reason for everything. You thought there were trolls on the roof, remember? And there was a reason for that.'

'What's that awful smell?' Elf said suddenly. 'It's like . . .' she wrinkled her nose. 'It's like a *bad egg*, isn't it?'

Olaf sniffed the air, and frowned again. 'I recognise the smell,' he began. 'I know! The hot pool where we bathed. The steam smelled a bit like this. Remember when you said that there were giants inside the mountain, heating up the water with a big fire?'

'I thought you didn't believe in giants.'

'I don't. But there must be a big fire around here somewhere to make all this ash. And something must make the water hot. So maybe there is a fire in the mountain.'

'Then Unn's right! There are giants!'

Olaf shook his head. 'That noise and the shaking, and the ash, and the smell. They've all got something to do with it. I wish I could work out what was happening.'

Next day it was still raining. The pastures around the summer farm were squelchy and sodden, and all the streams and waterfalls were white and foaming, and roared much more loudly than before.

Shortly after rising time, Elf was sitting in the covered dairy milking Audumla the cow, when Olaf burst in looking very wet, bedraggled and agitated.

'Elf, come quickly!' he called.

'What's the matter?'

'It's the sheep. The ewes. They've all gone . . .'

The Lost Sheep

Elf left her milking and ran to join Olaf by the sheepfold. He was staring at the empty square of hoof-trodden mud and shaking his head.

'I can't understand it,' he said. 'We left them shut in didn't we? Last night, when we were in here talking?'

'I think so. And the gate's still closed. They must have jumped over. Perhaps they were frightened by all those noises.'

They spent all morning searching for the ewes. First they looked in the birch woods and down along the river. Then they climbed up along the crags almost as far as the glaciers. In the afternoon they walked all around Rettafell mountain and up on to the bare moor above the valley. By mid-evening time when they were forced by hunger and exhaustion to return to the homestead, they had still found no trace of the missing animals. Sheep were grazing happily all over the fells, but not a single ewe. Olaf was despondent and really worried now.

Next day Elf persuaded Hildi to take over the milking for her, and joined Olaf in his search.

'I'm sure we'll find them today,' she said confidently.

Olaf did not look as if he shared her optimism. 'We'll have to take a couple of the ponies,' he said. 'We'll never find them otherwise, they might be anywhere on the mountains by now. I wish Asjolf were here. He'd know what to do.' He tossed a stone angrily into the mud.

It was another damp, mizzling morning, with the moisture hanging thickly in the air. They could not see much farther than the coppice of small birch trees down by the river, and the glaciers and fells were shrouded in dark clouds.

'I wish this weather would clear,' Olaf said dismally, as he fetched some rope from the farmhouse. 'We'll never see anything if it stays like this.'

They set off up the valley and eventually found the ponies on the pastures directly below the glaciers, where they had first learned to ride. But they seemed disturbed by the strange noises from the mountain which had started again that morning. The whole herd was wheeling round, manes and tails flying.

Olaf dropped his rope to the ground. 'How are we going to catch them if they're running up and down like that?' he said despairingly, as the ponies wheeled round in front of them. As usual, Freyfaxi led the herd.

'*Bokki! Bokki*!' Elf cried, and ran after the ponies a little way, but still they did not stop.

'What are you calling *him* for, Elf?' Olaf shouted angrily. 'Are you crazy? We can't ride that one in broad daylight. Somebody might see us.'

'I thought if I could get Freyfaxi to stop, then the others might. He's their leader, isn't he?'

They watched helplessly as the ponies galloped around the pastures. The broad valley looked completely different from the enchanted place they had known. Mist and cloud hung over the crags, and the waterfalls, which had looked like silver cobwebs in the night-time sunlight, were now dirty torrents, vomiting mud and boulders from the glaciers.

'We'll just have to keep on walking,' sighed Olaf.

They trudged wearily across the ridge on the far side of the pasture, and came down on the other side. Olaf thought the ewes might have got mixed up in the flocks of sheep belonging to their neighbours.

Here there was another summer farm, with other flocks and herds grazing on the pastures. All the sheep in this valley were branded with a red mark, using the dye from the madder plant which grew plentifully in this part of Iceland, but they could see none bearing Sigurd's brown 'S' mark. They stopped at a hut and asked the shepherd if he had seen their missing ewes.

'No, can't say I have,' he replied without much interest. 'Where are you from, Sigurd Asgrimsson's place?' He glanced casually at Olaf. 'Lost them have you?' Olaf nodded. The man carried on whittling a piece of stick into the shape of a shepherd's crook. 'Then you'd better find them quick, my fine *bokki*. Old Sigurd killed one of his shepherds once. Just up there, on the other side of that ridge.'

Elf glanced round at Olaf, who had turned pale.

'When did you lose them?' the man asked him.

'I found they'd gone yesterday morning. They must have run off in the night.' The man whistled between his teeth, as if he did not reckon much on Olaf's chances of survival. He shook his head.

'Could be halfway round the glaciers by now. Or dead at the bottom of a ravine somewhere. Scared by the noises, more than likely. You heard them?' They nodded 'Giants,' the man said. 'You see that mountain up there?' He pointed towards the topmost heights of the glaciers, where a dazzling snow peak just showed between the dark clouds. 'They call that "Odin's cauldron". They say there's a great lake of boiling water up there, bubbling away under the ice. I don't know whether that's true or not, but I've heard some mighty strange noises coming out of that mountain, and it scares me, I can tell you.' The shepherd stared up at the mountain top, shaking his head, then turned abruptly to Olaf. 'How many did you say you'd lost?'

'Twenty eight. All ewes.'

'You can't be such a bad shepherd then, if you know how many's gone. There's many that wouldn't. If I get a sight of them I'll come over and tell you,' said the man, who told them that his name was Eyvind. He seemed after all to be quite impressed by their determination to find the missing flock.

'Thank you for your help,' said Olaf. They plodded wearily back across the ridge, leaving the shepherd still whittling his stick and shaking his head.

As they trudged up the slope towards the farm, Olaf was grim-faced and looked on the edge of despair. 'They're probably all dead by now,' he said wearily. 'We'll never find them.'

'Yes we will. I'm sure we will.' Elf always wanted to look on the bright side of things. 'Let's look in the sheep-fold. They might have come back by themselves.'

They hadn't.

By the fourth day of their searching they had been all over the surrounding fells several times and even Elf was beginning to think that they might never find them.

'We can go up around Rettafell again,' Olaf said despondently. 'Maybe we missed them in the rocks somewhere.'

'Maybe we did. Maybe we'll find them today.' Even as she spoke, Elf knew that neither of them really believed it any more.

As soon as they got up into the mountains they seemed to walk right into the clouds, which were clinging thickly to the lower slopes. After a while they could hardly see their hands in front of them, and began to slide and stumble on the loose stones. They decided to go back to the farm until the weather cleared.

It was now the hour of *dagmal*, three hours after rising time, when the first main meal of the day was eaten. With any luck they would get something to eat before setting off again.

Rannveig, dressed in a hooded cloak, was standing outside the farmhouse talking to some of the girls. She seemed to have a friend with her for there was a strange girl standing beside them, holding the bridle of a black pony.

'So you have lost all my father's ewes, slave-boy,' Rannveig called out scornfully, as Olaf and Elf came up to the farm. 'It is all up with *you*, for certain. My father will cut off your head now.' She smiled maliciously.

'I have come up with my friend Halldis to choose a couple of nice ponies for our journey to Hofdabrekka. But it seems they are all running wild too.

'Well, Halldis, it seems we are not to have ponies after all, and will have to make do with these lazy creatures. We have made this journey for nothing.' She turned to the other girls. 'You will prepare a meal for us, and after that we will return to Thorolfsfell.'

While Rannveig and her friend were treated to a dish of salmon inside the summer farm, Elf and Olaf sat outside and ate some cold meat and blood-cake. They stared gloomily into the mountains, where every so often a patch of crag or ice showed through the fleece of cloud, and then vanished again.

By the time they had finished eating, it looked as if the clouds might lift. The wind was freshening, and they could see patches of sky above the peaks. Rannveig and her friend emerged from the house.

'How I shall look forward to seeing my father cut off

your head, slave boy,' said Rannveig airily to Olaf as she came out of the house. She and her friend climbed on to their ponies.

'Look!' Elf shouted suddenly, standing up and pointing towards the mountains. 'I can see them! There! There! See? Right up by the glacier!' The wind had really freshened now, and the clouds had lifted from the surface of the glaciers. Far up on the mountain, right underneath one of the overhanging tongues of cracked ice, was a group of black dots.

Olaf shielded his eyes against the glare from the ice. 'They're just rocks, aren't they!'

'No, no,' Elf insisted. '*They're moving.*' Everybody had rushed outside and now peered up towards the crags.

'It *is* them!' Olaf cried, suddenly feeling a wild excitement.

'Now what are you going to do?' Rannveig put in spitefully.

'We need to take one of the ponies, and some rope. Asjolf told me . . .'

The pony herd was grazing only a short distance away from the summer farm, and Olaf immediately ran down the slope to try and get hold of one of them. But it was no use. As soon as they saw him coming they all tossed their heads nervously and galloped off across the valley. Olaf chased them for some distance, but in the end he had to give up, and trudged back to the farmhouse.

'We'll never catch up with them without a pony,' he said despairingly. The clouds had come down again, and Olaf knew that every moment which passed lessened their chances of finding the ewes. It would take them hours to get up on to the mountain without a pony.

'Don't think you can borrow one of *our* ponies,' Rannveig said quickly. 'They are not to be ridden by slaves, and besides, we need them to go back to Thorolfsfell. We are late already.'

At this moment Elf noticed that Freyfaxi had separated from the rest of the herd, and was bounding up the slope towards them at a high-stepping, *tolt* pace. He stopped about a stone's throw away from them, snorting and tossing his mane.

'He wants to help us,' Elf whispered to Olaf. Olaf said nothing. Neither of them noticed the cunning smile which now spread over Rannveig's features.

'Why do you not ride that horse, slave boy,' she said, indicating Freyfaxi with her riding whip.

Elf and Olaf looked at each other.

'We can't,' Olaf muttered. 'He's a sacred horse . . .'

'Oh, my father will not mind about *that*,' Rannveig replied airily. 'Not if you get his sheep back for him.' She turned. 'Come along Halldis, we have a long ride back to the home farm. We'd best be on our way.'

Elf and Olaf watched in silence as Rannveig and her friend trotted away across the slope.

'What are we going to do?' Elf said, as soon as they had gone out of sight around the overhanging cliffs at the head of the valley.

'We can't ride him, Elf. The master said he'd kill anybody who did. I heard him. So did you. He meant it.'

'You said he'd kill you if you didn't find the sheep. He can't kill you twice can he? And think how pleased he'll be if we *do* find them, Olaf. You heard what Rannveig said. I'm sure Sigurd won't mind us riding Freyfaxi as long as we can get his ewes back for him.'

Olaf frowned, as if he were carrying on a great struggle in his mind. Then he went to fetch the long length of knotted rope which Asjolf had told him he would need in case any of the sheep had got themselves stuck in the rocks.

'All right,' he said grimly, when he came back. 'I've got to find those ewes. I suppose this is my only chance. Sigurd will kill me if I don't find them, I know that.'

Elf held the pony steady for him, but Olaf still hesitated.

'I'll come with you,' Elf said. 'Freyfaxi will easily be able to carry both of us. He's very strong.'

Olaf shook his head. 'It's all right. I'll go alone. Why risk your life as well, Elf? I've got to. I'm the shepherd.'

'I'm not going to leave you *now*, stupid. We've been through worse things than this together.' Olaf looked at her, squeezed her arm for a moment, then climbed on to Freyfaxi's back.

Elf hauled herself up in front of him, patting the pony's neck. 'See, nothing happens,' she said.

'Come on then,' Olaf said gruffly. 'Let's go.'

'See how the slaves ride my father's pony!' Rannveig said excitedly, watching them from behind the crags at the entrance to the valley. 'I knew they would, the stupid creatures. How I hate the pair of them. Remember that you have seen it too, Halldis, for we must now hurry and tell my father. He loses sheep every year but he never goes back on an oath once he has sworn it. He will cut off both their heads now, for sure.'

Rannveig flicked her pony with her riding whip, and led the way down the steep track towards the home farm.

At the Precipice

Up on the mountainside Elf and Olaf had located Sigurd's sheep and rounded most of them up into a gravel hollow. But three of the ewes were trapped halfway down a cliff on the other side of the ridge, and several more had got up on to the glacier itself.

Like real mountain shepherds, the two children were now working on equal terms with their dogs and pony. The dogs, Frekki and Brokk, had known exactly what to do, and the rescue party would never have reached the sheep in time had it not been for Freyfaxi's speed and surefootedness. All the ewes had seemed intent on following their three companions down the cliff face, and when they had finally caught up with them, the stupid animals were already pushing and shoving each other towards the edge of the precipice.

'Come on, Elf!' Olaf shouted.

She hurried to catch up, stumbling across the loose boulders, and leading Freyfaxi by the forelock.

'There they are,' Olaf said, pointing down the cliff face. The three ewes, bleating miserably, were perched on a ledge some way below them. 'There's nothing else for it,' the boy muttered determinedly. 'I'll have to go down.' He took the coil of rope from his shoulder. The rope had knots tied all along its length, about an elbow's length apart. This was so that it would not slip, and made climbing down on it much easier.

Olaf tied one end of the rope securely round Freyfaxi's stocky body, exactly as he had been taught by the old shepherd. 'Do you think he'll know what to do?' he asked Elf.

'Of course he will. Won't you *bokki*?' Elf patted him. 'Stay still, stay still . . .' Freyfaxi shifted on his hooves, but seemed to understand what was expected of him.

Olaf looped the other end of the rope securely round his own body. 'Here I go.' He walked to the edge of the precipice and peered over. The black cliff fell sheer into a narrow gorge, where the rocks had been torn and twisted into strange shapes by the ice and the torrents. Above, to his right, wrinkled fingers of dirty-looking ice reached down towards him from the glacier. The trapped sheep bleated from the ledge.

Olaf lowered himself over the edge of the precipice nervously. How the sheep themselves had managed to get down on to the ledge he had no idea.

The first part of the cliff was quite easy. The frost and snow had ripped and cracked the rock so that there were good hand and footholds. Then quite suddenly the piece of rock he was holding on to split away and he fell backwards into space.

Above, the rope tautened suddenly. Freyfaxi slid back on his hooves, but managed to keep his footing.

Olaf's hands slid down the rope and the jolt winded him, but he managed to grip on one of the knots and hung on desperately, kicking his legs in the air. He was terrified. He swung round dizzily, trying not to look down to see how far he would have fallen. He swallowed, and waited for a moment until his heart stopped racing and the rope stopped swinging.

'What happened?' Elf called out.

'It's all right. I slipped.'

Olaf started to climb down again, this time relying on the pony to take the weight while he gingerly felt for footholds on the cliff. He looked down. There was a stretch of smooth rock just below him, with nothing to hold on to at all. Then there was a drop of about three times his own height, and he would be on the ledge. He tried not to panic.

'Look after me, Freyfaxi,' he muttered, then put all his weight on the rope and began sliding down, one knot at a time.

'Steady *bokki*,' Elf said, gripping the pony's mane and holding on to his halter. Again Freyfaxi shifted on his hooves, but took Olaf's entire weight without much difficulty. Elf shivered. The wind was moaning round them, bringing with it the cold breath of the frost giants from the mountains above. The strange rumbling sounds had started again.

Suddenly the rope went slack. 'Elf! I'm down on the ledge! I'm going to try and get one of the sheep!'

There was a narrow cleft with a loose scree of small stones a little way along the cliff. Olaf started to make his way carefully along the ledge, keeping hold of the rope, and trying not to make any sudden movements in case he frightened the ewes.

'Come on, girl,' he said softly. The nearest ewe began to scrabble its way up the cliff but Olaf managed to get a grip on the damp wool of its coat and, although the animal bleated and struggled, it soon gave up and went limp.

Exactly as he had been taught, Olaf tied the end of the rope underneath the ewe's forelegs.

'It's all right, girl,' he murmured, to comfort the animal. 'Elf!'

'Yes?'

'I'm ready! He can start pulling now!'

Elf began to lead the pony away from the edge of the cliff.

'Come on, *bokki,*' she said gently. As soon as he felt the weight of the sheep behind him Freyfaxi knew what was required and began to haul gamely on the rope.

Slowly, the sheep began to rise up the face of the cliff. At one point it started to swing round on the end of the rope, kicking wildly and showering Olaf with dislodged stones, but although Freyfaxi's hooves slid and stumbled, the strong little pony kept on pulling and pulling.

At last, the ewe's head and forelegs appeared over the edge of the cliff. Its head was lolling with exhaustion, and it looked more dead than alive. Then, hearing the others bleating in the hollow, it seemed to revive and began to scramble over the top. Elf ran to help.

'We've done it!' she shouted to Olaf, who was now standing very confidently on the ledge. She untied the rope from around the ewe's body and called one of the dogs.

'Frekki! Frekki! Here boy! Here!'

Leaving the other dog to mind the rest of the sheep, Frekki bounded across the scree of boulders, and began yapping at the heels of the rescued animal.

'Good boy,' Elf gasped, falling to the ground. 'Good boy, take her in, that's it.' The ewe gave a final kick, then ran to join the other sheep in the hollow, chased by the barking sheepdog.

Rescuing the other two ewes was no easier. But at last they had all three ewes safely up.

'How many have we got?' Olaf asked breathlessly, as he clambered to safety over the top of the cliff.

'Twenty-eight. We did it! We did it!' Elf exclaimed happily. They hugged each other in triumph, and patted the dogs and the pony.

Olaf sighed with relief. He could not believe that his master would punish them too severely for riding the pony, not after what they had done. Everything, he was sure, would turn out all right in the end.

'Are you sure we've got all of them?' he asked, suddenly anxious again. Elf counted them again.

'Quite sure,' she said. 'Every last one of them.'

Troll-Cleaver

Olaf was wrong, of course. As soon as Rannveig had told her father that she had seen the slaves riding the sacred pony, Sigurd had called for his axe.

Ignoring the pleadings of his wife, he saddled up a pony and set off up the valley towards Godaland, with the great axe 'troll-cleaver' strapped across his back. When he reached the first ford, he saw his son Skamkel riding across from the opposite bank, leading a line of ponies which were piled high with sheafs of hay.

'Skamkel!' Sigurd bellowed. 'I have need of you!'

'I see you are carrying your axe, Father,' Skamkel said, looking Sigurd up and down with some amazement. 'And yet you are not wearing a helmet.'

'I have no need of a helmet for this business!' Sigurd replied. He explained what had happened.

'I see,' sneered Skamkel, 'This is certainly an heroic exploit. And you need my help in killing these two unarmed infants, Father, is that it?'

'Don't take that tone with me!' Sigurd barked. 'I take no pleasure in this business; they were good slaves. But they have insulted the god, and therefore they must die. I need you as a witness, that is all. Afterwards we will announce the killings and that will be the end of the business.' Skamkel shrugged his shoulders, and rode off with his father in the direction of the glaciers.

The ride to the summer pastures was never an easy one, and that day their progress was slowed even more by the many fords, for the mountain torrents had been swollen by the days of rain. So it was well towards mid-afternoon when Sigurd and Skamkel finally rode into the valley of Godaland and trotted up towards the summer farm.

The girls were busy churning butter in the dairy, while Unn recited her usual litany of spells against the trolls. Sigurd summoned everybody outside and demanded in thunderous tones to know where the slaves could be found.

'They've gone to rescue the sheep,' Hildi told him.

Skamkel tapped his father on the shoulder and pointed up the valley.

Coming down across the pastures were the bleating ewes, with the sheepdogs running round them. The two young slaves followed behind, leading Freyfaxi by the halter.

Sigurd leaned on his axe, looked coolly at Skamkel, and waited.

'They found them!' Hildi exclaimed admiringly.

Olaf and Elf were so exhilarated by their success that they were not as careful as they might have been about coming close to the farmhouse with the forbidden pony, and they led him right up to the sheepfold. While Olaf drove all the ewes back into their pen, Elf led the pony around to the front of the summer farm.

'There you are, *bokki*,' she said to him. 'I'll just take your halter off, and then you can have a good roll in the grass.' Then she looked up, and stopped short. Sigurd was standing a short distance away, glaring ferociously at her. In his hand was 'troll-cleaver', his mighty axe. Skamkel stood beside him, with his usual sneering expression. Nobody said a word. Nobody moved.

Elf felt her legs go weak underneath her. Surely Sigurd did not mean to kill them. Not after what they had done . . .

'Where is the boy?' Sigurd said grimly.

'Olaf?' Elf replied faintly, trying to give herself time to think. *He really does mean to kill us*, Elf thought. *What shall I do*? She made a sideways movement, but Skamkel quickly caught hold of her. At that moment Olaf came round the corner of the diary with the sheepdogs running at his heels.

'I counted them again,' he said cheerfully. 'Twenty-eight . . .' Suddenly he stopped short and stared at the two men. The girls looked on, terrified.

The silence was broken only by the rhythmic churning of Unn's butter churn, and her ceaseless chanting. 'The wolf is loose, the fire is coming, the giants are coming. Jormungand, Surt, Ratatosk, and Nidhogg!'

'You have been riding my horse,' Sigurd said slowly. Olaf, too, felt that his legs were about to give way. He glanced at Elf. Their fate had closed in upon them.

'Which horse, Master?' he stuttered.

'Do not play at chess with me, boy! That horse! That one there! The horse which is sacred to the god Frey. My daughter Rannveig saw you. She came to tell me of it.'

The snake, Elf thought.

'You have disobeyed me. He is a sacred horse, and you have insulted the god! Do you understand what that means?'

Elf and Olaf glanced at one another. Then Olaf said, 'All the ewes went missing, Master. We were afraid they would go over the cliffs and die. Unless we had a pony we could never have got to them.'

Sigurd nodded. 'And my ewes?' he asked.

'We saved all of them, Master. Three of them had gone down a cliff.'

'You have done well. But why did you not take one of the other ponies? I was fair with you, boy. You knew of my oath, that I would kill any person who dared to ride this animal. You knew that this was a sacred horse. I told you that you were free to ride any of the horses in Godaland, excepting only this one. And yet this is what you have done.'

Olaf did not reply.

'We didn't hurt him!' Elf blurted out suddenly. 'He wanted us to ride him. He almost asked us, even the first time . . .' She drew in her breath, aware of what she had said.

'*The first time*!' Sigurd shouted, rounding on her furiously. 'Then this is not the only time you have ridden the sacred horse?'

Olaf gave a strangled cry and closed his eyes.

Freyfaxi was standing a few paces away, watching everything that was going on. His ears were pricked forward and he was staring intently at Skamkel, who was still holding on to Elf, a cruel expression on his face. Freyfaxi had sensed that Elf was being threatened.

'It was me,' Elf shouted. 'I was the only one who rode him before. Olaf never did. He never wanted to, not even to look for the sheep. I made him do it. None of the other ponies would let us near them. We tried to catch one of the others, but they ran away.'

Sigurd said nothing, but his eyes blazed with fury.

'We did get all your sheep back for you. We couldn't have done it without Freyfaxi . . .'

'*You* had no right to ride any of the horses, slave-girl! You are not my shepherd. Your task is in the dairy, and yet you rode the sacred horse. You encouraged the boy to do so?'

When she did not reply, Sigurd struck her on the cheek making her cry out.

'You mock my gods! You are a follower of this White

God, like my son Kari! You have deliberately disobeyed me!' Sigurd turned to Olaf. 'You, boy, I would spare, if I had not sworn my oath. You have done well to save my ewes. You would have made a good shepherd. If you had not listened to the evil tongue of this slave-girl, this would not have happened.'

Sigurd got a good grip on the handle of his axe, flexing it in his hands, and took a sight on Olaf's neck as if he were about to fell a small birch tree.

'Ready boy?' he asked grimly. 'You shall be first.' Olaf nodded.

Elf could not bear to see Olaf accept his fate so meekly.

Suddenly she screamed out, 'What's wrong with riding a horse? Run, Olaf! Run!'

'Hold your tongue!' Sigurd roared.

Everything then happened very quickly.

Sigurd, in a fury, turned towards Elf, swinging his axe behind his shoulders, meaning to strike her instead. The axe blade flashed. Elf screamed. Skamkel, afraid of being sliced in half himself, let go of her. At that moment Freyfaxi let out a squeal of rage, laid back his ears and charged straight at Sigurd, knocking him sideways. The axe blade embedded itself harmlessly in the turf wall of the summer farm.

Elf ran. The danger, and her own anger, had kept all her senses as sharp as Sigurd's blade. Yelling at the top of her voice, she ran to Olaf and grabbed him by the hair.

'Come on, you idiot!' she screamed at him. '*Run*!'

Freyfaxi wheeled round and reared up, kicking savagely at Sigurd with his front hooves.

'Get the horse off me, curse you!' he called out to Skamkel.

Skamkel began to jab at the pony with his short-sword, but this only enraged the animal even further. Squealing and snorting, his nostrils flared and his mouth flecked with foam, Freyfaxi now turned on Skamkel.

'Get off! Get off!' Skamkel shouted, as the pony pursued him around the farmhouse, rearing and kicking and rolling his eyes in fury.

Sigurd managed to avoid the flaying hooves and wrenched his axe out of the turf. But his head was bleeding, and one of his eyes had hooded over.

Elf was pulling Olaf back towards the sheepfold.

'Come on!' Elf cried, and they scrambled across the yard and clambered on to the stone wall. '*Bokki*! Here!'

Freyfaxi was still chasing Skamkel around the farmhouse. As soon as he heard Elf's voice, he turned and galloped over the grass towards them. They both managed to leap on to his back when the pony drew level with them.

Elf, who was sitting in front, squeezed Freyfaxi with her knees. 'Go on *bokki*, go!' she yelled. The pony needed little encouragement, and galloped off down the slope towards the stream. Cursing, Skamkel gave up the chase and ran back towards the summer farm, nursing his bruises.

The yellow outline of Freyfaxi, with the two slaves on his back, could be seen clearly moving up the side of the ridge on the far side of the valley. 'You let them go, you numbskull!' roared Sigurd angrily at his son. 'Are you going to stand by and see the gods dishonoured? Help me to my horse, curse you!'

Skamkel helped his father into the saddle. 'You're getting too old for all this oath-taking and vengeful killing, Father. Can two brats now defeat the great Sigurd Asgrimsson?'

Sigurd glared at his son for a moment without speaking. Then he pulled his horse round and set off in pursuit of the escaping slaves.

The Outlaws

'Are they coming?' Elf shouted, as she urged the pony up the slope. Olaf glanced behind him. He could just make out the summer farm.

'I can't see anybody.'

When they reached the top of the ridge they paused for a moment, and looked back sadly at the green valley below the glaciers. Then they began to trot down the steep slope into the next valley, through a sparse coppice of tiny dwarf-willow trees which hardly reached as high as the pony's chest. There was no cover, nowhere to hide. Ahead of them they could see the shepherd named Eyvind, driving some ewes into his sheepfold.

'Don't say anything to him,' Olaf whispered into Elf's ear. 'He's bound to tell Sigurd.'

'Did you find your sheep?'the man called out as they rode past.

'Yes thank you,' Elf replied, without slowing down. They could not afford to take any chances.

'Where are you off to now?' he asked.

'Back to Thorolfsfell!' Elf called out. She kicked her legs gently and the pony was soon prancing away at a smart *tolt* pace.

'That's never the way to Thorolfsfell!' Eyvind shouted, but they were already on their way up the next ridge. 'Now I wonder why they're going off in such a hurry?' he said to himself.

He did not have to wait very long to find out, for shortly

after this Sigurd and Skamkel came riding over the top of the ridge, and reined in beside the sheepfold.

'They passed me not long ago with their horse all in a lather,' Eyvind told them. 'Going east towards the glacier tongue. Though I can't see what they'd be wanting up there. I thought they'd found their ewes.'

'I'll go on ahead,' Skamkel said to his father. 'If you follow the river round you can head them off as they come down. They won't go up on to the glacier.' He dug his sharp spurs into the flanks of his pony. The animal, a chestnut stallion, was already exhausted by the ride up from the home farm and was foaming at the bit. 'Go on you brute!' Skamkel shouted, and jabbed the pony savagely again with the spurs. It began to move off up the hill.

Sigurd turned to Eyvind. 'Get me a fresh horse, and come along with me. I want those slaves caught tonight.'

Eyvind hesitated. He resented being ordered about, but like the rest of the poorer farmers in the district, he depended upon the powerful Sigurd for support in his own disputes.

'You had better do as I say, Eyvind Bjarnarson,' Sigurd barked at him, 'if you want my support against Lodmund Ulfsson at the next assembly.'

Eyvind shrugged his shoulders. 'As you like,' he said.

'There's somebody coming up the ridge now,' Olaf called out. 'It looks like Skamkel.' He was peering down from behind a large boulder, while Elf and Freyfaxi hid themselves over the crest of a bluff. It was now mid-evening time.

They remounted the pony, and continued along the screes of gravel and boulders just underneath one of the glacier tongues. The going was difficult, and after a while the pony began to pant and wheeze heavily.

'What are we stopping for?' Olaf said in alarm.

'We're not stopping. I'm slowing him down. He's tired, he's been carrying us for hours.'

Olaf looked back over his shoulder. 'They'll catch up with us soon,' he said desperately.

'He won't be able to go on much longer, Olaf. Just look at him.' The pony's coat was damp and steaming with sweat, and although he tossed his head and carried gamely on, it was clear that he was badly in need of rest. Elf patted his neck. 'We'll have to find somewhere to hide until he's rested.'

In front of them, a wrinkled slab of dirty ice jutted out from the main glacier, blocking their path. They skirted the edge of the ice, crossed a shallow torrent of foaming melt-water, and came down on to a rocky pasture. Here there were a few sheep grazing on the meagre grass, so Elf halted the pony to let him feed while they tried to work out what was the best direction to follow.

'What are we going to do?' Olaf wailed.

Ahead of them, barren sheep pastures clung to the slopes of the ice packs. Away to the north lay the jagged black summits of the interior, bleak and desolate. The barren mountains of Iceland were no place to be alone, hungry and friendless.

Hooloolooloolooloo!

They looked up. A flight of wild grey geese was passing overhead, silhouetted in a 'V' formation against the bright northern sky.

Elf thought, *They're going home for the night. Everybody's got somewhere to go except us.*

'Look!' Olaf said, suddenly gripping her tightly around the waist. 'Riders! Down there!'

Two horsemen were coming up towards them, following the course of one of the glacier torrents. They were some way away, but the leading rider looked like Sigurd. They both scanned the desolate landscape with their eyes, trying to find somewhere to hide.

'What are we going to do?' Olaf moaned again.

All the time they hesitated, the riders were drawing nearer and nearer. And they both knew that Skamkel must be even closer behind, somewhere on the other side of the glacier.

'This is all your fault!' Olaf burst out, almost in tears. 'If I hadn't listened to you, none of this would have happened.'

'*Shut up*!' Elf hissed. 'We've got to hide somewhere!' She sniffed. 'Look down there. There's a wood. Maybe it's big enough to hide in.' Far away to the east, beyond the glaciers, a large river glinted in the evening light, and they could see patches of green clinging to the valley slopes on either side.

'Let's try it,' Olaf muttered.

By the time they got to the woods midnight was approaching, and the whole land had taken on the strange, colourless aspect of a northern summer night. They dismounted at the edge of the trees. The coppice was dark and shadowy, and they could hear rustlings coming from among the leaves.

It was not really the sort of wood that Elf was used to. The tree trunks were no thicker than her forearm, and there was no real undergrowth, just grass and weeds, and the odd boulder. They hid themselves and the pony as best they could behind some rocks, and peered back through the half-darkness.

Elf turned to Olaf and whispered. 'I can hardly see you at all.'

'Let's hope they can't either.'

Shortly after midnight Skamkel reached the coppice. Sigurd and Eyvind the shepherd were quite close behind.

Olaf and Elf flattened themselves on to the ground. They could hear the men moving through the coppice, only a short distance away.

Skamkel was now within twenty paces of the runaway slaves. He stopped and looked around him. The twisted, silvery trunks of the trees reflected the eerie light. Skamkel did not see the eyes that looked at him through the flickering shadows. He saw only what looked like an empty coppice, and walked on. Elf and Olaf began to breathe again.

Sigurd and Skamkel moved away through the trees. Then they moved off out of sight, and presently the fugitives heard them getting on their ponies and riding away.

'I'm hungry,' Elf whispered, when they dared to speak again.

'There's a hut over there, through those trees. There might be some food in there.'

'Supposing somebody comes?'

'I don't suppose anybody will, not now. Not until the morning.'

The hut was in a clearing where the trees had been felled all the way to the edge of the copse. There were several charcoal stacks dotted around the clearing. Wisps of smoke rose into the air from the stacks, which were covered over with turf to keep them burning slowly.

Inside the hut it was very dark and damp. The floor was covered with pieces of wool fluff, muddy and blackened with charcoal. Olaf found a cloth bundle on a shelf at one side of the hut and opened it.

'Cheese,' he said. 'We're in luck.' He broke off some

large chunks of the white cheese, which was made from ewes' milk. They ate hungrily.

'I hope he won't mind,' Elf said with her mouth full, catching crumbs of cheese with her cupped hand. 'Whoever this belongs to, I mean.'

'Too bad if he does. We're outlaws now, aren't we? If we want to eat we'll have to steal.'

Elf thought about this, then said dismally, 'But we can't just go on living like this for the rest of our lives.'

'What else can we do?' Olaf yawned, exhausted suddenly. 'There's nowhere we can go.'

'Why don't we go to Kari?' Elf brightened suddenly. 'Kari wouldn't give us up, not ever. I know he wouldn't.'

'But where is he?' Olaf mumbled sleepily.

'Oh – he told me. It's where the Christians are. Wait . . .' Elf searched her memory for the name of the place where Kari had gone, but it wouldn't come back to her. Finally she gave up, lay down on the floor beside Olaf and closed her eyes.

The Charcoal Burner

Tok Tok Tok.

Elf opened her eyes. She had been dreaming.

Tok Tok Tok.

There was the sound again.

She sat up suddenly. They had slept right through the night, and it was now full daylight!

'Olaf! Wake up! It's morning!'

Olaf stirred slightly. 'Olaf,' she hissed in his ear. 'I think the charcoal burner's here. It's daylight!'

Olaf was suddenly fully awake.

'Olaf! There's a man out there and he's sure to come to the hut to have his breakfast. Of cheese. Which we've eaten!'

The chopping noise stopped. It was already too late for escape. Just in front of the hut, the woodchopper was standing with his back to them, carrying a bundle of logs on his shoulder. He was a very tall man, with red hair, wearing a striped tunic and a woollen cap. He seemed very puzzled by the sight of a small pony looking at him from the other side of the clearing.

'What's this then?' the woodcutter said to himself. Then he turned and saw them.

The man stared at the two figures in astonishment. Then he leaned down to take a better look at them. Elf held on tightly to Olaf's sleeve.

'Mother of Loki!' the man exclaimed. 'It's the saxon whelp, and the other one with her!'

It was Thorfinn Redbeard.

'Running away are we?' he said slowly with a significent glance at their slave collars.

There was nothing for it but to explain what had happened to them and how they came to be in the hut. Before Elf had finished her story, Thorfinn suddenly stood up, listening alertly.

'Somebody's coming,' he muttered. He quickly looked around the clearing, then walked across to the only charcoal stack that was not smoking, and heaved up the turf which covered it. 'In there,' he said curtly. They hesitated. 'Hurry up. This one's all burned through by now. It won't hurt you.'

Elf and Olaf clambered inside and squashed themselves down on to the crackling bed of charcoal. Thorfinn quickly replaced the layer of turf over their heads, then strolled casually over to a pile of logs, and began chopping them into short lengths.

Half-crushed by the weight of the earth and grass on top of them, the runaway slaves waited to see what would happen.

'How do we know he won't give us up?' Olaf whispered.

'He won't.'

Olaf grunted and tried to make himself more comfortable, as a sharp piece of charcoal was digging into his hip. He knew from bitter experience that the Viking kind were only interested in money or treasure. Thorfinn might be a charcoal burner for the moment, but he was still a Viking at heart. There was usually some sort of reward for capturing escaped slaves, and he could easily make himself some extra silver out of them if he was clever. Elf didn't seem to realise that, Olaf thought bitterly. Elf trusted everybody.

Soon they heard the jangling of bridles, and the sound of ponies trotting into the clearing.

Freyfaxi's out there! Elf remembered suddenly. They

had forgotten about him in their scramble to hide themselves. What if they recognised him! She twisted herself round, and managed to get a grass-fringed view of what was going on, through a gap in the wall.

Skamkel and three other men had ridden into the clearing. Freyfaxi was nowhere to be seen.

Skamkel dismounted, and once more scanned the coppice for any sign of the runaways. He and Sigurd had headed on around the edge of the glaciers for several hours the previous night, but had lost all trace of the slaves. So, while his father rode from farm to farm, getting a huge search party together, Skamkel had decided to retrace his steps in the hope of picking up their trail again.

Thorfinn paused in his work, leaned on his axe, and said, 'What brings you to Miklafell wood so early in the morning, Skamkel Sigurdarson?'

Skamkel continued surveying the clearing, as if he were sure that the runaways were hiding close by. 'Do I know you, fellow?' he asked, without bothering to look at Thorfinn.

'You won two ounces of silver off me at the horse fights last month.'

'Did I? I don't recall you.' Skamkel walked over to the hut, looked inside, then slowly made a circuit of the clearing. Elf, in the charcoal stack, swallowed in fright. The noise sounded so loud in her throat that she was sure Skamkel would hear her. Olaf shifted his position slightly, and the brittle charcoal underneath him crunched loudly. Skamkel was passing at that very moment. Elf could see his calfskin boots through the gap in the turf. But he seemed not to hear anything.

A pony snorted in the wood. Both of them knew it was Freyfaxi.

Skamkel looked round sharply, but saw only the vague

outline of a pony munching at the dwarf-birch leaves some way into the coppice. Listening out for any tell-tale noises in the trees, Skamkel walked over towards the edge of the wood. Thorfinn, seeing that he might get close enough to recognize Freyfaxi, hurried after him and barred his way.

'Is it firewood you're after, Skamkel Sigurdarson!' he said, fingering the handle of his axe. 'My master's had enough trouble this year with the thieving of firewood. If you want any, go down to Myrdalsand and collect driftwood.'

Skamkel turned on him with an arrogant sneer. 'There are four of us, woodchopper, and if we wanted firewood we'd come and cut it down, and you with it. As it happens, we don't. We're looking for two runaway slaves that have stolen a horse. Brats, about so high. Could be they're hiding among your precious trees.'

Thorfinn relaxed his grip on the handle of his axe. 'Oh, is that all?' he said, as if firewood thieves were his only concern. 'Two riding on a single pony, would that be them?'

Skamkel nodded very slightly. 'So, you *have* seen them, woodchopper. Well, where are they?'

Thorfinn hesitated. 'What's it worth?' Skamkel clicked his fingers. His three companions strode across the clearing. They were all big men, armed with swords and axes. Two of them grabbed Thorfinn's arms while the third dug the sharp point of a sword into his ribs.

'I'll tell you what it's worth, woodchopper,' Skamkel said coolly. 'Your life. Because if you don't tell us, I'm going to split you into two pieces all the way down from your red hair to your fancy cowhide boots.'

'I saw them as I was riding up here,' Thorfinn muttered, as if the information was being reluctantly forced out of him. 'Heading north up the right bank of the river. You'll catch them if you hurry.'

Skamkel nodded, and signalled to the men to release Thorfinn. Then he climbed on to his pony. 'There's four marks of silver on their heads, woodchopper,' he said. 'But we want them alive. It is my father who must kill them.'

Thorfinn whistled, and slung his axe over his shoulder. 'Four marks! What have they done, murdered their master's wife?'

Skamkel dug his spurs into the flanks of his pony. 'They have offended against the god Frey. They have purchased their deaths.'

Thorfinn watched the men ride away. As soon as they had gone out of sight beyond the trees, he walked over to the charcoal stack where the frightened pair were hiding and pulled back the turf. 'Get into the hut,' he said gruffly, gesturing with his thumb.

Elf and Olaf climbed out and glanced at each other uneasily. Their clothes and faces were now covered in charcoal smudges, and they looked like real outlaws of the mountains. They walked into the hut. Something about Thorfinn's tone of voice frightened even Elf. Olaf had never trusted him anyway.

They sat down on the floor of the hut. Thorfinn followed, blocking out the light from the entrance. He had some lengths of rope in his hand, and a very grim expression on his face. He sat down on the large boulder which served as a chair, but did not look at them.

'Thank you,' Elf said.

'For what?' Thorfinn fingered the rope in his hand.

'For not giving us up.'

Olaf's eyes flicked between the two of them in the

shadows. Everybody's breathing appeared to be unnaturally loud.

Thorfinn grunted. 'Only a fool would have done that. There's four marks of silver on your heads, you know that? Four marks. Do you think they'd have paid out that sort of money if I'd given you up there and then?' He shook his head. 'Anybody who catches you, if he's got any sense, is going to tie you up and hide you up on the fells, somewhere nice and safe. Then, if he's still got any sense, he'll go to Asgrimsson and tell him straight out, "No money, no slaves." He's got to pay up then.'

Olaf uttered a stifled cry and scrambled towards the entrance. Without even turning his head, Thorfinn caught hold of the boy in a strong grip, and pulled him back.

Elf's voice came from the shadows. 'It's all right,' she said, 'he won't give us up.' She and Thorfinn stared at one another without moving.

'What makes you so sure?' Thorfinn burst out at last. He seemed really angry. 'What makes you think I owe you anything? I spared your life, you saved mine. That makes us evens. I need those four marks, curse you!' Elf did not take her eyes off his face.

'The trolls take you!' Thorfinn shouted. 'You saxon witch! Take your spell off me! I need those four marks!'

'I know you won't give us up,' Elf said quietly. Olaf, still struggling vainly to escape, felt Thorfinn suddenly relax his hold on him.

'Curse your luck!' Thorfinn shouted, and flung the pieces of rope out through the doorway with an angry gesture. He shook his head. 'There goes my last hope of getting back on the ships. I'll never get away from this place now.' After cursing the ground for a little while, he suddenly appeared to relent and reached down two of the cloth bundles that were stacked away on the stone shelf behind him. Seeing that most of the cheese had been eaten already, he looked at them both significantly, but said nothing.

'Here,' he said, cutting off some slices of blood-cake that he'd brought with him that morning. 'When things look at their blackest, get some food and drink inside you. That's what we always used to say on the ships.'

Elf and Olaf ate the blood-cake hungrily. It tasted dry and fatty, and neither of them really liked it, but it made a very welcome breakfast all the same.

'Gulp it down, whelps,' Thorfinn said. 'You haven't got much time.' He took a swig of ale from a goatskin sack, then handed it to Olaf. 'I may have got rid of them for a little while, but they'll come back, and when they do you've got to be well clear of here.'

Olaf took a mouthful of strong, bitter-tasting ale. His eyes started to water and he choked slightly. This seemed to amuse Thorfinn, who slapped him on the back.

'Steady lad, easy does it.' The Viking took the ale sack out of Olaf's hands and handed it to Elf. 'Well now, whelps, have you any sort of plan in those heads of yours, or are you just going to keep on running like scared rabbits?'

'If only we could find Kari . . .' Elf began.

'Kari Sigurdarson?'

Elf nodded. 'He'd never give us up,' she said hopefully.

'That's right enough, seeing as he risked his own life to save you once before. So where is he, do you know that?'

Elf frowned. She took a long sip of ale and wiped her mouth with the back of her hand in imitation of Thorfinn. 'Kirk . . . Kirk something . . .'

'Kirkubyr?'

'Yes! Yes! That's it!' Elf's eyes were shining with excitement.

Thorfinn nodded. 'That makes sense. They're all followers of that new God of yours over at Kirkubyr. He'd be there, right enough.'

'Is it far?' Olaf asked, beginning to feel hopeful again.

'About a day's ride south-east from here, by the direct route down the valley. You'd have to stay well up towards the glaciers to avoid meeting anybody, so it could take much longer. And it's the worst direction you could choose to head in, because there'll be a big search party out looking for you by now, and you'd risk running right into them, going down that way.'

Elf and Olaf looked rather crestfallen, but Thorfinn suddenly stood up and reached down his wooden shield from a shelf under the roof.

'It's still worth a try,' he said. 'It's the best chance you've got, and with a bit of your Saxon luck, we might just get through. Bring all the food.'

He strode out of the hut. Elf followed.

'You said "We". Are you coming with us then?' she asked.

'That's right, whelp. It's Thor's will we should try our fates together, I'm sure of that now. You've brought me luck once, maybe you'll bring me luck again. Where's that horse of yours? Run and catch him. We'd best be off, seeing as we've got a start on friend Skamkel. He thinks you're heading north. You, boy, what's your name. Can you handle a sword?'

Olaf looked at the ground. 'No, Master.'

Thorfinn grunted. 'When I was your age I was as tall as a man already and had killed three men. You can ride though?'

'Yes, Master.'

'That's something. I've got two pack ponies over in the wood there. You can ride one, I'll take the other, and the saxon whelp can take that horse of yours that's caused all the trouble.'

Elf scampered obediently across the clearing and into the wood. She could not believe the sudden change in their luck. She did not even mind being called a saxon whelp. Coming from Thorfinn, it did not seem to matter.

She called Freyfaxi to her and led him into the clearing to join the others.

'Ready, whelps?' Thorfinn said, and he swung himself on to his pony's back. 'We haven't got much of a chance, I can tell you that now, but we'll give those farmers a run for it before they get us.' He held out his arms in front of him, making the sign of the hammer.

'May the thunder-god protect us!' he called out to the sky, and the three of them set their ponies' heads in the direction of the bleak mountains to the north.

The Waters of Odin

Thorfinn seemed amazingly cheerful and even sang as he rode, but Elf did not share his high spirits.

They were crossing a sloping pavement of black lava-rock, which was riven with cracks and fissures, and covered with patches of frost and ice. Every so often the wind drove flurries of dirty snow across the rocks, which whipped into their faces, hard and painful, and made them all shudder with the cold. They were very close to the ice cap now.

'There's that noise again,' Elf said, urging on Freyfaxi to catch up with the others. The strange rumbling sound, which they had heard so often before, was once more echoing over the desolate ice slopes above them.

'It's definitely not thunder is it?' Elf persisted. 'More like a lot of giants throwing hundreds of rocks about.'

'Shut up, Elf,' said Olaf.

In a gulley they found a stream and a patch of sickly lyme grass. Thorfinn dismounted. 'Best let the beasts feed while we can, whelps. There's not a lot of grass on these mountains. Not a lot of anything.'

As the ponies grazed Thorfinn cut off some slices of the blood-cake for them all to eat, and they took a drink from the stream. The water tasted bitter and brackish, but was very welcome. Then they heard the rumbling noise again. Elf swung round.

As she did so, a tongue of flame shot into the air from the very top of the great ice-mountain, the one that Eyvind had called 'Odin's cauldron', which now towered directly above them.

'The ice is on fire!' she cried out in horror. 'Olaf! Thorfinn! The ice is on fire!'

The others looked up, but the shining summit of the mountain was once more shrouded in dark clouds. Olaf sighed.

'Oh, Elf! Things are bad enough already. I suppose you're going to tell us you saw trolls lighting bonfires.'

'The ice was on fire. I saw it!'

'You can't have done. Ice doesn't burn. It's only frozen water, and water doesn't burn.'

'I *did* see it! You never believe anything I say. Not ever.'

'Come on, whelps! No quarrelling among comrades. Haven't you got enough enemies already?'

As they continued across the dark rocks, Elf glanced uneasily at the ugly shaped rocks all around them. The whole lava-field must have flowed out of the side of the mountain during some great volcanic eruption, long ages before; the rock itself still looked like oozing black mud and had set, hard and sharp, into strange and frightening lumps.

'*Troll-daughter, fell-walker, touch me not, touch me not,*' Elf muttered under her breath, so that Olaf would not hear her.

'Odin's ravens!' Thorfinn exclaimed suddenly, pulling his pony up short. Just ahead of them, on the side of a scree of cinders, was a strange, cone-shaped mound. A thick stream of bubbling mud was oozing out of the top of the cone, melting the ice around the base, and staining it a sickly yellow colour. As they watched, horrified, the whole mound began to hiss and steam, and then vomited out a great fountain of mud and water.

The ponies reared up in terror, and the three of them

shielded their heads under the hoods of their toggle-cloaks.

'What's happening?' Elf shrieked, pale with fright. A strange, clinging vapour with a smell like rotten eggs hung thickly in the air, making their eyes water, and the sky had gone dark. It began to rain ashes.

'Mother of Loki! What is this?' Thorfinn cried out, brushing a hot cinder from the sleeve of his tunic. The ponies were whinnying in pain now as the glowing ashes scalded their coats. Elf was screaming.

'Cover the ponies' heads!' Olaf yelled, trying to make himself heard above the rumbling noise from the mountain, which was growing louder every moment. He seemed to be the only one of the three who was keeping his head.

The dark clouds around the summits of the ice mountains were now lit up by flashes of lightning, and they could hear real thunder now, which sounded quite different from the muffled rumbling of 'Odin's cauldron'. Then, louder than anything they had yet heard, a vast crackling sound issued out of the murk at the top of the mountain. The clouds parted and they saw the lurid red glow of giant flames playing around the summit.

'It's the fire giants!' Elf yelled. 'I told you . . . it's the fire giants!' She was crying now. The rain of ash had intensified, enveloping them in a swirling cloud of red-hot cinders. They were all coughing and choking from the fumes, and frantically trying to brush the cinders from their clothes and their ponies' coats. Thorfinn was white-faced and shaking. It was the first time Elf had ever seen him frightened.

'Mother of Loki,' he stammered, 'the gods are angry . . .'

'It's because of us,' Elf sobbed. 'Isn't it? Because of what we did.'

'No it isn't!' Olaf shouted over the din. 'It's got nothing to do with us or anybody. It's just happening. I don't know why, but it's just happening!'

Seeing the boy's lack of superstitious fear, Thorfinn suddenly sat up straight in his saddle, ashamed of his own terror.

'Come on, whelps,' he said gruffly. 'We can't stay here, we'll have to go down off the mountain.'

They all jumped off their ponies and scrambled down the side of a steep scree of cinders and gravel. When they were clear of the worst of the falling ash, they paused for breath.

'It looks as if the gods are on Sigurd's side after all,' Thorfinn said wryly, 'since they seem to be driving us right into his hands.'

They heard another muffled explosion on the mountain behind them, and the sky was once again lit up with a red, flickering glow.

'Sigurd hasn't caught us yet,' Olaf said doggedly.

Thorfinn looked at him, a grim smile playing on his lips. 'Right enough, boy, right enough. And I'll send a few of those farmers' sons to Asgard before they *do* catch us, I can promise you that.' He swung himself up into his saddle and turned to Elf. 'Let's be moving. With a bit of your Saxon luck, we might just slip through their fingers.'

'I think I've used it all up by now,' Elf replied bleakly.

'Riders!' Olaf cried out. 'Coming this way!'

Four horsemen had appeared over the top of the ridge ahead of them. Although they were still some distance away, there seemed to be something familiar about them . . .

'It's Skamkel!' Elf gasped. 'I'm sure it is! I know the way he sits on his horse. He's realised we tricked him.'

'Curse our luck!' Thorfinn muttered. 'Wheel about whelps! Let's try and get behind that bluff over yonder before they see us!'

They pulled their ponies round and began to *tolt* across the waterlogged ground towards a grassy hillock which might give them some cover. Too late, they realised that they had ridden into a patch of bog.

'He's sinking! Freyfaxi's sinking!' Elf shrieked, as the pony floundered and squelched in the greeny-yellow scum.

'Let them find their own way across!' Thorfinn shouted.

Elf and Olaf loosened their reins, and found that the animals seemed to know instinctively which parts of the mire were safe, and which were treacherous. Even though their ponies' legs sank deep in the ooze, their hooves always seemed to strike firm rock underneath, and before long they were safely across.

'They've seen us,' Olaf panted, as his pony scrambled up on to the firmer ground. Skamkel and one of his companions were already starting to cross the mire. The other two were heading off around the edge to head off their escape in each direction.

As they rounded the corner of the bluff, Elf drew in her breath. She could see immediately that the luck of the elves had well and truly deserted her.

'Sigurd . . .' she whispered.

About forty or fifty armed riders were spread out in a line across the whole length of the broad valley at the foot of the ice mountains. As soon as they caught sight of Thorfinn and the fugitive slaves they spurred on their ponies and began pursuing them at a gallop across the mud.

The three friends urged on their own animals, but the valley suddenly narrowed and they found themselves in a deep ravine from which there was no escape. Sheer black cliffs confronted them on three sides, whilc it was only a matter of moments before Sigurd's men caught up with them from behind. A short way ahead, a huge waterfall deluged over the precipice and tumbled into the ravine across jagged rocks.

'Down!' Thorfinn shouted, dismounting.

Elf and Olaf jumped off their ponies and flattened themselves on the gravel. They heard Sigurd's voice echoing off the cliff face behind them.

'Give up the slaves, Redbeard! We've got no quarrel with you!' Sigurd's men were already dismounting and fanning out across the gravel banks in the bottom of the ravine.

Thorfinn said nothing, and looked round quickly to check the lie of the land.

The sides of the canyon were so steep that the low-lying Icelandic sun never penetrated the bottom, and the ice still clung to the rock faces. A thick sheet of ice covered the rocks on the right-hand side of the falls, extending in an arched lip all the way to the edge of the torrent.

'Whelps!' Thorfinn hissed, buckling on his helmet. 'You see behind the waterfall? Look like there's some sort of ledge. If we can get behind it I might be able to hold them off single-handed. It should be easy enough to get to it across the ice.'

Olaf immediately began to scramble to his feet but Thorfinn pushed him firmly back to the ground.

'Not yet!' he barked. 'Wait till I give the signal. I'm going to try to make them rush at *me*. That was we stand a chance of making it on to the ice before they do. If we let them know what we're going to do, we'll never make it. Understand?'

Three of Sigurd's men started to run at them, brandishing shields and spears.

'Don't move yet, whelps,' Thorfinn muttered. 'I can handle these three.' He gripped his axe with his right hand, held his shield firmly in the other, and waited for the onslaught.

It never came. Instead, one of the men started waving his shield frantically and shouting. 'Hold off!' he cried. 'Put up your axe! We're with you!'

To Olaf's astonishment, he recognised Eyvind the shepherd from Godaland.

'I'll not stand by and see this done,' Eyvind said breathlessly, as he took up a position beside Thorfinn. 'Not while I've still got a good sword arm. They're good bairns, they don't deserve to die, not for this.'

Thorfinn nodded and raised his axe in a gesture of salute. 'We're going to try and make it across that ice and behind the waterfall. We'll lock shields until we get on to the ice. Wait for my signal.' He threw another glance at Sigurd's men who were spreading out, getting ready to attack.

'Olaf, come here boy, and take my shield. I'll need both hands for my axe.' Olaf crawled over to him. 'Just grip it tight,' Thorfinn told him, 'by the leather pad, there. Go on boy, it's not heavy. When your friend here moves, move with him.'

Gripping his axe firmly with both hands, Thorfinn stepped outside the wall of shields. 'Here they come,' he grunted. 'Don't move until I give the word.'

The attackers now came running in force, some with large battle axes, others with swords and shields, or long halberd spears with barbed prongs. Thorfinn waited until they were halfway across the gravel bank of the river.

'Now! Run!' he shouted. The wall of shields began to move. Olaf slipped on the gravel, but Eyvind pulled him up. Somehow Olaf managed to keep his shield locked against the others, and ran on.

Where's Freyfaxi? Elf thought suddenly, as she stumbled along behind the shield-bearers. She tried to look over the top of the line of shields, but could see only a confused mass of helmets and cloaks. Several ponies were galloping loose but she could see no sign of the little stallion.

The attackers were on them now, hacking and thrusting, trying to break the wall of shields.

Crunch!

One of the shields split.

Ting! Ting! Ting!

Swords rang together. Men yelled and roared. Axes flashed. Blood splashed on to Elf's arm.

Then the shield wall broke and they were up and running along the bank of the foaming river. They could hear men shouting in confusion and agony, and ponies whinnying as they smelled blood and death.

Elf reached the sheet of ice, but several of Sigurd's men had got there before her. She tripped and fell as one of them made a grab at her. She slid right underneath the legs of two of the men, then rolled heavily against another's leg. This man grabbed hold of her arm, and shouted, 'I've got one of them!'

'Get the other one! Take them alive!' Elf recognized Skamkel's voice.

Then, quite suddenly, she became aware of horsemen galloping across the gravel, of other warriors leaping off their mounts and joining in the fighting. On their side!

One of them grabbed the man who was holding her, forcing him to let go. In another moment the man had toppled backwards across the ice and dropped screaming into the swirling torrent below the waterfall. Elf felt herself being lifted up and pushed across the ice. She looked up and saw that her rescuer was wearing a silver helmet and a scarlet tunic . . .

'*Kari* . . .!'

'Get across, Elf!' he shouted. 'Olaf! Quick! They're right behind you!' Kari ran back across the ice to fight off two of Sigurd's men who were almost on to Olaf.

'Get behind the waterfall!' Kari shouted. He pushed Elf and Olaf along the narrow ledge which led right behind the tumbling sheet of water until they were out of sight of their pursuers.

Several of Kari's followers and Eyvind made it across the bridge of ice and formed another shield wall across the ledge.

Thorfinn was still hacking his way towards the river, felling Sigurd's men as if they were the birch trees in Miklafell wood, and roaring like a madman. He had a terrible wound in his side, and was bleeding badly. Skamkel and a great mass of Sigurd's men pressed in on him, trying to dodge in underneath the whirling axe blade, and give the huge Viking his death blow. Thorfinn reached the bridge of ice, and turned to face his attackers.

'Why doesn't he follow us?' Kari shouted.

'*Go!*' cried Thorfinn. 'I'll only slow you down now! Save the whelps, Sigurdarson! I'll hold them off until I go down!' He swung his massive axe around his shoulders in a last desperate stand, as a huge onslaught of Sigurd's followers poured on to the ice bridge. Skamkel himself hung back, pushing the other men across the ice to face the flashing axe-blade. Many more fell at Thorfinn's hands, tumbling into the foaming chasm below the ice bridge, before the great red-bearded Viking himself went down, wounded and exhausted.

Skamkel, once he was quite sure that Thorfinn was no longer able to lift his axe, walked across the ice to give him his death blow.

'Now you will see how I fell trees, woodchopper,' he sneered, raising the blade of his own axe high above his head. 'Like *this*!'

Thorfinn Redbeard's great body slid slowly from the ice bridge and vanished in the foam below.

'We'll never hold them!' Eyvind cried. More and more of Sigurd's men were now pouring across, and Sigurd himself now appeared behind them, wielding his great axe 'troll-cleaver'.

Kari ran back along the ledge until he could see Sigurd, advancing behind the press of warriors.

'Stop this madness, Father!' he shouted above the din of the waterfall. 'Is this your religion? All this useless killing? How many more have to die before your gods are satisfied?'

In answer Sigurd brandished his axe at Kari. 'Only the slaves!' he bellowed. 'Stand aside and let me have them!'

'Elf! Olaf! Run!' Kari called out. Sigurd advanced and aimed a blow at him. Kari deflected the axe with his sword, but lost his balance and tumbled down across the slippery rocks. Elf screamed. Kari vanished in the spray below.

At this moment the second shield-wall broke and Sigurd's men began surging along the ledge. Eyvind went down under the weight and took a glancing blow on the side of his helmet. With a cry, he too plummeted into the waterfall and disappeared.

Then, quite suddenly, everybody stopped moving and

looked up. The whole rock face had begun to tremble and shake, and an unearthly roaring sound echoed around the walls of ice on the mountains above them. As if forgetting the battle which had so concerned them only moments before, Sigurd and his men gazed upwards with superstitious horror. Plumes of fire and belching clouds of smoke and steam had appeared around the summit of 'Odin's Cauldron'. Then, as the mountain finally awoke from its frozen sleep, gigantic fragments of melting ice began to split away from the eastern flanks of the summit. With a deafening rumble the pent-up waters inside were suddenly released, and a great flood swept down the side of the mountain, bringing with it an avalanche of mud, sand, ice and boulders.

Seconds later, a colossal wave surged over the cliffs and into the ravine. Sigurd was immediately swept away in the flood. The ice platform cracked and split, and floated off in the torrent, taking with it about twenty of Sigurd's men including Skamkel.

Elf and Olaf flattened themselves against the overhanging rock just underneath the waterfall. Several huge boulders and large blocks of ice bounced down the mountainside over their heads and crashed into the water in front of them, followed by a cascade of liquid mud and sand. They had brief glimpses of men's helmets and horses' heads sweeping past them in the foaming water. Then a second wave of floodwater roared down the gorge.

They clutched on to one another. The torrent engulfed them, and Elf felt herself being wrenched away from Olaf by the force of the deluge. She screamed, took mouthfuls of muddy water, and was swept away in the flood.

River of Fire

Elf was paddling desperately, trying to keep afloat, but she could feel that her strength was going. A dead body floated past, tumbling limply in the foam. Elf went under. A boulder crashed into the water just beside her, narrowly missing her head as she came up again. Exhausted, she gave up struggling against the current and was swept down the valley.

Then, ahead of her, she saw a group of ponies swimming towards the dry ground. She caught a glimpse of a familiar, sandy coloured head. Freyfaxi . . .

'*Bokki*! Here, *bokki* . . .' With a last frantic effort she splashed towards the swimming pony. She went under again. But Freyfaxi had heard her voice, and swam towards her, lifting his head above the spray and baring his teeth. Somehow Elf caught hold of his mane, and at that moment felt all the strength go out of her.

The pony struggled towards the bank of gravel, with Elf hanging on weakly to his shaggy mane. By the time they reached the solid ground the waters had subsided, leaving in their wake a desert of oozing black mud, criss-crossed by thousands of trickling rivulets. Boulders littered this wasteland, together with the corpses of men and horses.

Elf lay for a long time, exhausted, on the edge of this desolation. Then she felt Freyfaxi licking her face.

She staggered to her feet. She had no idea where she was, as the flood had washed her some way from the scene of the fighting. Then she heard again the terrible crackling noises from the mountains above her.

She looked up towards the summit of 'Odin's cauldron', and let out a cry of horror.

The whole of one side of the mountain had split open, and vast quantities of a red-hot, oozing sludge were now pouring out. Rivers of orange flames seeped down across the slopes, sending up billows of hissing steam as they cut their way through the ice in their path. Clouds of ash and cinders swirled over the crags, while fountains of crimson fire rose and fell into the air all along the great cracks in the rock.

It's the end of the world . . . Elf whispered. Unn had been right after all. The Doom had come.

Turning her face away in terror from the glare of the fires, she saw a dark shape moving along the edge of the swollen river.

There's somebody else! Elf thought excitedly. *Somebody else is still alive!* Waves of relief rose up inside her, and she ran eagerly along the edge of the mud. The man rose to his feet. He had a helmet on his head, and a muddy axe in his hand.

The smile of relief faded from Elf's lips.

It was Sigurd.

He limped along the gravel towards her. He had seen her, and recognised her. Elf was close enough to see his crazed expression. He still meant to kill her . . . She couldn't believe it. *The world was ending.* Nothing mattered now.

She began to scream and ran blindly away from him. Out of the corner of her eye she could see two other figures coming towards her. It was as if she had never stopped running, ever since the day she had fled from her burning village. This was how it had all started. And this was how it was all going to end.

She could hear Sigurd shouting wildly behind her.

'Frey! Odin! Cease your anger! Stop the flames! See, I am here! I shall avenge you!'

'*He's mad*, Elf sobbed to herself. It doesn't matter now . . .

Suddenly she realised that Freyfaxi was bounding along beside her. The faithful little pony had not deserted her. Elf paused for a moment. She was in one of the steep, narrow gullies that ran up the side of the moutain. What was she going to do? It was certain death to go back, she knew that. Either Sigurd would get her, or one of the others she had seen behind him. Go on then. Up the gulley. Up towards the fire giants and the burning mountain . . .

She grabbed hold of the slimey coil of rope which was still tied around the pony's neck and hauled herself up on to his back. Freyfaxi began to scramble up the gulley. Once again the amazing sure footedness and courage of the Icelandic pony came to her aid. Although the air was thick with fumes and falling ash, Freyfaxi clopped steadfastly on, and they began to draw away from Sigurd.

'Up there *bokki*.' She guided the pony up a steep ledge to get clear of the poisonous fumes which were collecting in the bottom of the gulley.

They emerged from the shelter of the rocks on to an open pavement of black rock. Waves of sound and heat buffeted against them like a solid force. About three hundred paces ahead the great gash in the mountain was spewing out a mixture of glowing lava, and bubbling black sludge. The roaring noise was deafening.

Bouf! Bouf! Bouf!

Fountains of blazing lava suddenly spurted into the air all along the wall of flame.

Screaming, Elf slid to the ground and pulled the pony under an overhang of rock, trying to shield his head with her dripping cloak. She pulled the hood tightly over her face. Small pieces of red-hot pumice and cinders started to float down all around them.

'Oh, *bokki* . . .' she whimpered, burying her face in his mane.

When the storm of ash cleared a little, Elf could see clearly that a great river of glowing sludge was heaving its way across the mountain towards her. A smaller stream of lava had already started to pour into the top of the gulley to her right. There was no way through. This was the end.

Boom! Boom! Boom!

Blazing fragments of rock shot into the air. The whole mountain was shaking now.

Then Sigurd appeared out of a cloud of ash. He was bellowing out the names of his gods but his voice was drowned by the noise of the eruption.

Bouf! Pieces of blazing pumice bounced off the cliff behind Sigurd and showered down on his helmet. He staggered, but still came on.

Elf screamed, 'We can't stay here *bokki*! Come!' She made a last desperate effort to get past Sigurd. The ground was shaking so much now it was difficult to keep upright. The noise and heat were overwhelming. Sigurd tried to hit her with his axe, but the movement overbalanced him. The whole rock face shuddered and lurched. He slipped backwards, and pitched over the edge of the gulley.

'*Elf! Elf!*'

She turned, somebody was running across the rocks towards her, holding the hood of his cloak over his face. It was almost dark now. She couldn't see who it was. Then there was a brilliant flash of orange light as a fountain of lava exploded into the air behind her.

'*Olaf!*' She ran and hugged him, shaking her head in disbelief. 'How did you find me?'

'I came looking for you! I saw you down by the water! I waved at you but you ran away!'

Both of them had to shout as the noise from the eruption almost drowned their words.

'I thought you were one of Sigurd's men! That's why I ran away!'

'One of them followed me, but I got clear of him. What's happened?'

'It's Sigurd . . .'

They both peered down into the gulley. A river of boiling lava was advancing down the narrow cleft, hissing and crackling. Sigurd lay on the bare rock at the base of the cliff, directly in the path of the flow. He seemed unable to move, but they knew he was still alive because they saw him move his arm slightly.

Elf and Olaf looked at each other, uncertain what to do.

Bouf! Bouf!

They clutched each other tightly as another rain of ashes showered down around them. Then they looked down the gulley again. Suddenly, everything had changed. Sigurd was no longer the fierce avenger of the god Frey. He was a helpless human being lying in the path of the monstrous heap of bubbling lava that every moment was drawing closer and closer. He was Kari's father. Gunnhild's husband. Their master still . . .

Elf turned to Olaf and shouted over the deafening noise, 'What are we going to do? We can't just stay here and watch it eat him up! I can't bear to watch it, Olaf!' She was screaming now, and had buried her face in Olaf's cloak. Olaf tried to keep calm and work out how long it would be before the lava flow reached Sigurd. It seemed to be moving at about the speed of a man walking, and was already only about eighty paces away from him.

'It's no good, Elf! Our only chance is to pull him back up the cliff. And we can't. It's impossible!'

Elf suddenly raised her head. '*Yes we can*!' she yelled. 'We can, Olaf! Look, Freyfaxi still has the rope round his neck . . . the one we used to rescue the sheep . . .'

Olaf ran across to the pony and started unwinding the rope. Without a word he began to secure one end around Freyfaxi's body, exactly as he had done when they rescued the sheep.

Below, the hissing flow of red lava and cinders pushed itself another few paces along the bottom of the gulley.

'Olaf!' Elf shouted. 'I'm going to come down with you! Freyfaxi knows what to do now.'

Olaf nodded without turning to look at her. He completed his knots and quickly tested them for strength, patting Freyfraxi as he did so.

Elf took his arm suddenly. 'Olaf . . .' she said anxiously, 'is this the end of the world?'

'No, of course it isn't. The inside of the mountain's on fire, that's all.'

He lowered himself over the edge, payed out the rope from his left hand, and bounced down the cliff face. The rope was still slimey from the floodwater, but the knots prevented him from slipping too fast.

Boom! Boom! Another shower of cinders.

'Stay still *bokki*! That's it. You remember!' Elf patted him. The pony shifted on his hooves and found places in the rock to steady himself. He remembered.

Olaf's feet dropped on to the bare rock at the bottom of the gulley. 'All right! I'm down!'

Elf slid down the rope to join him. The wall of smoking lava now towered above them, only about thirty paces away. As they ran towards Sigurd, the searing heat hit their faces making them both cry out.

'He's still breathing!' Olaf yelled. Sigurd was slumped on his back over a fissure in the rock. Olaf began knotting the rope under his armpits. Both of them were coughing and choking from the fumes and ash.

Sssssssssssss . . .

A rivulet of orange, liquid rock trickled ahead of the main flow, coursing rapidly along a fissure. Straight towards Sigurd's foot. Elf screamed and tried to move his leg. She tugged desperately and his foot came out of the boot. Moments later the lava trickled over the tough cowhide and melted the whole boot with a loud hissing noise.

'*Now! Go!*' Olaf yelled to Freyfaxi. He tugged on the rope. The pony immediately began to pull against the weight, remembering what they had done on the mountain when they had rescued the ewes. Sigurd was much heavier than a sheep, but Freyfaxi was very strong.

'Good *bokki*! Go on, pull! That's it!'

They each grabbed one of Sigurd's arms. Coughing, choking, they pulled as hard as they could. Sweat was rolling off their faces. The heat was almost unbearable. But Sigurd's body did begin to move, slowly.

They got him to the base of the cliff. Then he seemed to get stuck.

'What's happening?' Olaf yelled in alarm. 'He's not moving!'

'Pull *bokki*! Pull!'

No use. One of the knots had stuck against a protruding lip of rock on top of the cliff. They tried yanking at the rope but it wouldn't budge.

Sssssssssssss . . .

The flow was creeping faster now down the cleft towards them. Orange serpents of lava trickled out of the front. The whole heap bubbled and heaved, making a terrible crunching and crackling sound.

Elf climbed nimbly up the side of the cliff. She managed to free the rope. She ran to the pony and urged him forward.

'Come on, *bokki*! Pull! Pull! Pull!'

A fragment of hot ash landed on Freyfaxi's coat. Maddened by the pain and the heat and the noise, the pony heaved and pulled, but nothing happened. Sigurd seemed to be wedged into the rocks at the bottom of the gulley.

Bouf! Another explosion on the mountain sent cascades of sparks and pumice fragments into the air towards them.

'Help me, Elf! I can't move him!' Olaf shielded himself under his cloak from the shower of ash and rock.

Elf slid down the rope again.

Olaf pulled . . .

Elf pulled . . .

The pony pulled . . .

But still nothing happened. Sigurd's shoulders were wedged tightly into a cleft in the rock. The more they pulled the more stuck he became.

At this moment, Sigurd opened his one good eye. He seemed to understand what was happening, and tried to move, but the effort was too much for him.

'It's no good!' Elf screamed. 'We can't save him! We can't stay here any longer!' The lava was nearly on them now. The heat was so intense they were afraid their clothes would catch fire of their own accord.

The lava towered above them, heaving up and crashing in on itself in a flurry of sparks and flame.

Sssssssssssss! Crunch! Crackle! Sssssssssssss . . .

'Up the rope!' Olaf yelled.

Then Elf suddenly found herself being lifted by a pair of strong hands.

'Up the cliff!' shouted a voice she recognised.

It was Eyvind the shepherd!

'Go on lad, hurry! Back up the cliff! Get that horse pulling!'

Eyvind managed to get Sigurd upright. Elf and Olaf scrambled up the cliff, which had plenty of hand and footholds.

The lava engulfed the great axe 'troll-cleaver' only a few paces from where Sigurd had been lying. The polished steel blade melted instantly.

Elf was on top of the ledge now. She ran to Freyfaxi, seized the bridle and pulled him forward. The pony took the weight and put all his strength into one last mighty effort.

'That's it, *bokki*! Pull! Pull!'

The rope was moving! Sigurd's body started to lift slowly up the face of the cliff. Eyvind pushed from below until he too was forced to jump to safety.

'We've done it!' Olaf cried. Sigurd was safely on the ledge! Eyvind struggled over the top. Everyone sheltered as another explosion showered blazing pummice into the air behind them. When the ash cleared they could see that the gulley below them had completely filled with the bubbling tide of lava.

'Let's get out of this!' Eyvind shouted. The three of them managed to get Sigurd up on to Freyfaxi's back. Then they began to retreat back along the ledge and down off the mountain.

The Judgement

'Asgrimsson! Can you hear me? These two bairns saved your life up there.'

They were sheltering in a cave, waiting for the eruption to die down a little. Eyvind had torn off some strips from his tunic and was winding them around Sigurd's injured leg.

'Here, lad, give me a hand with this.' Olaf held Sigurd's leg steady while the shepherd pulled the ends of the bandages tight. 'You understand that, you old fool? You tried to kill them and they saved your life.'

One of the old man's eyes opened. The other was covered with another makeshift bandage. He groaned hoarsely, and nodded his head. He seemed to understand.

'Freyfaxi's hurt!' Elf wailed suddenly. 'Look . . .'

As soon as he had finished tieing Sigurd's bandages, Eyvind had a look at the burns on Freyfaxi's coat.

'He'll be all right, don't you worry. We're tough, us Icelanders, Aren't we *bokki*?' He patted the pony. Freyfaxi made a wheezing noise, and nuzzled his face.

'I thought you were dead,' Elf said, wiping her eyes. 'At the waterfall.'

Eyvind grunted. 'Takes more than that to kill *me*.'

'I saw you,' Olaf said. 'I saw you behind me when I got out of the water, but I thought you were one of the Master's men. I thought you were after me.'

'And I saw both of you,' Elf put in. 'I thought you were *both* after me.'

After a while the noise from the eruption quietened, and the ash ceased to fall. Already it was well past midnight, and the sky was white with the light of dawn. They got Sigurd up on to the pony's back again, and pushed on down into the foothills. It began to rain, and all of them raised their heads to let the cool, refreshing water wash away the smudges of ash and cinders from their faces.

Soon they were crossing the waste of mud and boulders left in the wake of the flooding. Then, quite suddenly, a group of riders armed with spears splashed out of the murk and surrounded them.

Elf and Olaf were almost asleep on their feet, but through the confusion of squelching hooves and snorting ponies they were aware of harsh voices barking orders.

'It's them!' 'Get the slaves!'

'It's Asgrimsson, he's still alive!'

'Let go of them, you trolls!' Eyvind shouted. 'They saved his life!'

One of the men struck the shepherd across the face with the back of his mailed fist. Olaf and Elf were shepherded forward with spears pointing into their backs.

'What's happening?' Olaf whispered to Eyvind. They had been taken to a nearby farmstead and tied up against the roof posts in the hall. Several old men were standing in a group at one side of the hearth, talking amongst themselves. They all wore long grey cloaks trimmed with fur.

'They're the *Godi,*' Eyvind replied grimly. 'The priests. They still want Sigurd to carry out his oath.'

The old man himself was propped up on a pallet of furs and straw. One of the priests strode over to him. The man looked imposing, with a mane of long white hair and fierce, bloodshot eyes. His name was Valgard Odin's-priest.

'You have betrayed the gods, Sigurd Asgrimsson. They are angry. That is why the fire mountains have erupted. You must carry out your oath now, you understand, or something even worse will happen.'

Sigurd tried to speak in a hoarse, wheezing voice. 'I tried . . .'

'You tried and failed. Failed to kill two slaves. You, the son of Asgrim the Mighty. The people will laugh at us, you realise that? They will say that the White God has defeated you. You want us to lose our following in this land, Priest of Frey? *Kill them! Kill them now!*'

'They saved your life, Asgrimsson!' Eyvind shouted. 'Don't do it!' One of the men kicked him savagely and the shepherd doubled up in pain.

Olaf and Elf were untied and dragged in front of Sigurd.

'*Do it*!' Valgard hissed, pushing Elf right in front of the outstretched blade which Sigurd grasped feebly in his right hand. One of the other men ran forward, drawing his own sword.

'I'll kill the brats!' he shouted. Valgard caught his sword arm.

'*No*! He must do it. The gods will not accept the sacrifice from any other hand . . .'

Elf could feel the stare from Sigurd's one good eye burning into her, but no longer felt afraid. Instead there was an expression on her face almost of pity, as if he were a poor wounded animal whose agony she understood. As for Sigurd, he seemed to be looking at her for the first time as another human being, and not just a small slave, one of his possessions.

With a clatter he dropped the sword and sank back, groaning. 'They saved my sheep . . . they saved my life . . .'

'So? Does that make any difference? They're only

slaves.' Valgard leaned down until his grey beard brushed Sigurd's face. 'The law is on our side. They mocked the gods and therefore they must die. At your hands. You *must* kill them, Priest of Frey. You *must* perform the sacrifice here, in front of witnesses! I am summoning a council of all the priests. Lodmund Ulfsson, chief priest in these parts, will be head of the council and its judges. You must accept our vote, Asgrimsson, or we will outlaw you and all your family.'

By noon the hall was crowded with all the priests of Odin, Thor and Frey. The chiefs of the council were seated at long tables on either side of the hearth.

Suddenly there was a commotion at the door. Elf's heart lifted as she saw Kari, tattered and dirty, push his way through.

'What are you doing here, blasphemer?' jeered one of the priests of Odin. 'What has this got to do with you!'

'It had everything to do with me,' Kari shouted back. 'I brought these two to Iceland in the first place. I found them on a ship. I gave them to my father because I thought they would have a happy and useful life on our farm.'

'You are worried about the happiness of slaves?'

'I believe that everybody has the right to be happy, slave or free.' This brought another outburst of jeering and shouting. 'I brought them here,' Kari continued, raising his voice, 'and now I feel responsible for them. They have no parents to speak up for them. They are quite alone in the world.'

'They have ridden a sacred horse which they afterwards stole,' Valgard Odin's-priest said drily. 'That is all that matters. They have broken our laws.'

'They saved my father's life during the eruption of the fire mountains. Most people know about that by now.

They risked their own lives to do so. Are we going to reward them with their own deaths? Are those our laws?'

'The slaves *caused* the fire mountains to erupt in the first place, Kari Sigurdarson, you can't deny that. They offended the gods, so the gods made the fires. If we do not kill them now it will happen again and again until we do!'

'That's just superstitious nonsense!' Kari cried out. 'You think this is the first time that fire has come from the mountains? It has happened before and it will happen again.'

Valgard Odin's-priest pointed his long fingernail at Kari. 'You see! He denies that the fire mountains show the anger of the gods. Blasphemy! The two slaves are sorcerers! They deliberately set out to mock the gods!'

'That's not true!' Kari retorted. 'They are strangers to our customs. They had no idea what they were doing. Why don't you ask them? Surely they have the right to speak?'

Lodmund Ulfsson, head of the council, stood up from his place. 'I agree. Our laws allow everyone the right to defend themselves. Bring the slaves here.'

Elf and Olaf were marched to the centre of the hall and stood before the high table. Lodmund Ulfsson looked sternly down at them and began his questioning. First he spoke to Olaf.

'You do not deny riding the sacred horse belonging to your master?'

'No, sir.'

'And why did you do it?'

Olaf explained about the missing sheep, and how none of the other ponies would let them on their backs. The chief judge nodded. Despite his solemn expression, he did not have an unkind face.

'And that was the only time you rode the sacred horse?'

Olaf hesitated, and blushed guiltily. Elf came to his rescue.

'I rode him before that,' she said quickly. 'Olaf only rode him when we went to get the sheep.'

'How many times was this?'

'Five, six times maybe.'

'But you knew it was forbidden?' Elf nodded and looked at the ground. 'Then why did you do it?' She shrugged her shoulders.

'I don't know. I wanted to learn to ride.'

'None of the other ponies would have done?'

'Freyfaxi was my favourite.'

'One final question. Do you worship the god called the White *Kristr*.' Elf glanced at Kari for a moment.

'I used to. Before. Before I came here.'

'And do you now worship Odin, Thor and Frey, like your masters?'

Elf hesitated. What was she supposed to say? The whole assembly had gone quiet. She decided to answer honestly.

'No.'

'And you, do you worship our gods?' Lodmund Ulfsson looked at Olaf. Olaf shook his head. 'Not any more,' he said quietly.

'Blasphemy! From their own mouths!' shouted Valgard Odin's-priest triumphantly. 'They must die. The law demands it.'

'Silence!' Lodmund Ulfsson commanded. 'We have heard enough now. Do you wish to speak, Sigurd Asgrimsson?' Sigurd shook his head. 'Then let us withdraw to vote.'

The priests stood up and filed outside. Elf and Olaf remained where they were, bewildered by the proceedings. Kari came over and stood beside them.

'We thought you'd been killed . . .' Elf whispered.

'I'm a strong swimmer, Elf, Don't you remember? I took a bad bump on the head, and didn't remember much till this morning, when I heard about the Council of Priests. News travels fast in Iceland – that's how I heard that my father was hunting you, and why we followed him till we found you.

'What's going to happen to us?' she asked anxiously.

'They're going to kill us,' Olaf muttered gloomily. 'You heard them. It's the law.'

'We're not beaten yet,' Kari said encouragingly. 'You both answered very well.'

'We said we'd done it,' Elf said. 'We admitted it.'

'You were honest, that's what matters. There's nothing disliked more here than somebody who starts coming out with whining excuses and says how sorry they are about everything. You answered well, both of you.'

'Well, we'll soon know what they've decided,' Olaf said with a hopeless air. 'They're coming back . . .'

The Lights of Elfheim

As the priests came back into the hall and went back to their places, Elf and Olaf clasped hands while Kari put a reassuring hand on each of their shoulders. Eyvind the shepherd glared around at everybody, while Sigurd lay still and stared in front of him.

The chief of the judges sat down in the high seat.

'Now hear the judgement of this council. *First*, we have decided that Sigurd Asgrimsson Frey's-priest acted within his rights according to the laws of Iceland in seeking the deaths of the two slaves . . .'

Sigurd turned to look at Kari, and slowly shook his head. His hand was trembling.

'*Second*!' Lodmund Ulfsson's voice echoed round the hall. 'We have decided that as they saved the life of their master, the two slaves have cancelled out the forfeiture of their own. The original oath made by Sigurd Asgrimsson concerning the horse Freyfaxi is therefore also cancelled without loss of honour.'

'What's happening?' Elf muttered in bewilderment. 'Does that mean they're not going to kill us?'

'I don't know,' Olaf said, equally bewildered.

'*Third*, we have decided that the slaves are not guilty of blasphemy against the gods since they have both admitted before this assembly that they are not believers in the god Frey. Therefore to them the horse was not a sacred object, and any insult offered to the god was unintentional on their part. And *fourth*! Although the act of the slaves in riding the sacred horse *may* have caused the fire mountains to erupt this can never be proved, and they cannot be put to death on these grounds alone . . .'

'Blasphemy! Blasphemy!' shrieked Valgard Odin's-priest. 'You'll see what will happen. Iceland will be consumed by fire!'

Lodmund Ulfsson ignored him and continued, 'We therefore find the slaves guilty of only one offence, the theft of a sacred horse, and we have fixed compensation as follows: forty ounces of silver to be paid by each of the slaves to Sigurd Asgrimsson, making a total of eighty ounces in all, to compensate him for the loss of his horse and the trouble they have caused. The horse in question has already been returned to him.'

'But we haven't got any money!' Olaf exclaimed in alarm.

'Let the slaves come forward.'

'Go on,' said Kari.

'You were both taken from your own lands against your will,' the chief of the judges began, 'and fate brought you to Iceland. We all know how you rescued your master on the mountains. We have also been very impressed by the way you have conducted yourselves at this council and answered all our questions honestly. We have therefore decided that we, the judges in this case, will pay the compensation in full.'

'Thank you, master,' Olaf whispered.

The chief judge stood up. 'Sigurd Asgrimsson Frey's-priest, do you accept this compensation?'

There was a moment of complete silence.

'I do,' Sigurd croaked. A great shout of applause went up. Surprisingly almost all the priests present had supported Lodmund Ulfsson. Only Valgard still raged and shouted, and prophesied doom and destruction.

Sigurd now rose slowly to his feet, leaning heavily on a

stick. He raised his right hand in the air and gradually everybody went quiet.

'I have done these slaves of mine a great wrong. They saved my life. And in what's left of it I'm going to try and make it up to them. So I want to announce before this council that I'm going to give them their freedom and adopt them into my own family as my foster son and daughter, with equal rights to my own surviving children.'

This was greeted with a tremendous cheer.

Sigurd limped forward and embraced first Olaf, then Elf, and then his son Kari.

As soon as Sigurd was able to travel, they returned to the home farm at Thorolsfell. Gunnhild ran out to hug them all and welcome them home, but Rannveig stayed sulking inside.

'I *shall* not call those creatures my brother and sister. I shall not do it! I shall go and live with my friend Halldis at Hofdabrekka and you will never see me again.'

The reunion of the family was not entirely happy, for Sigurd had lost his eldest son. Skamkel's body had been found half-buried in the mud when the waters receeded, and now he was brought back to Thorolfsfell to be buried next to his grandfather. Sigurd conducted the funeral according to the rites of Odin. Kari had hoped that his father might also adopt the new faith of the *Kristr*, but Sigurd said he was much too old to change his beliefs completely. However, he did annouce that he no longer objected to Kari worshipping whatever god he liked, and that he himself was giving up the worship of Frey in favour of Odin. This was a much simpler affair and did not involve any sacrificing, so from that time onward, the killing of horses and the eating of horsemeat died out at Thorolsfell.

As for Freyfaxi, Sigurd told everybody that as soon as he had been ridden he had ceased to be a sacred horse. He told Elf that she could keep the pony as her own, and Olaf could choose any of the ponies he liked from the herd up on the summer pastures.

As soon as possible the smith was ordered to remove the slave collars from Olaf and Elf. They had both become so used to wearing them, that their necks felt very odd once they had gone. It was as if something were missing from their bodies. The feeling soon passed however, and apart from losing their collars, there was little real change in their everyday lives. Elf was still expected to help with the milking and cheesemaking, while Olaf threw himself once more into his tasks as Asjolf's apprentice. He knew now that one day he would be the head shepherd, and Kari's most trusted helper when he took over the running of the farm from his father.

For the moment he was kept very busy with Asjolf, cleaning out and repairing the sheep and cattle byres at the home farm. The first snows had already fallen on the fells, and the time had come to round up all the animals, and bring them down from the summer farm.

But first, Kari announced, he had a duty to perform. He asked Elf and Olaf to ride with him to the scene of the battle by the waterfall. Thorfinn Redbeard, Kari said, deserved a proper Viking funeral, or he would never rest in his burial mound. The Icelanders believed that unless the dead were buried with proper respect, they walked inside their tombs.

The next day they set off with other members of the household across the mountain. Elf of course rode Freyfaxi, and the little pony was so happy to be out riding again with his friends that he tossed his mane, and frisked his tail, and snorted with contentment

It was a long, hard ride, as there was snow on the mountains, but they found Thorfinn's burial mound quite easily once they had reached the waterfall. It was marked by a simple stone carved with rune marks. Everybody helped to put up two lines of large stones around the grave, in the shape of a longship. This was the traditional way of burying a Viking warrior. Asjolf knew of an old man in the district who was a priest of Thor, and this man had agreed to ride over and perform the funeral ceremony.

This was a simple affair. The priest stretched out his arms across the grave, clenching his fists, so that he formed the sign of the hammer. Then he called upon the god to receive the dead Viking into Valhall, the great hall in Asgard where the chosen warriors were allowed to fight and make merry until the end of the nine worlds.

After the priest had gone, Elf lingered at the graveside, staring unhappily at the ship of stones. In the far distance, the last flickers of the eruption still blazed fitfully across the northern ridges. The lava flow had stopped now, and the mountains were settling down for their next long sleep.

'Come, Elf,' said Kari. 'There's nothing more to do.'

She was sitting on a rock, resting her head on her knees, and looking very sad. 'It was my fault,' she whispered. 'He was killed because of us. He said I brought him luck but I didn't. I brought him bad luck in the end, didn't I?'

Kari sat beside her and took her hand. 'Listen, Elf. I know it's difficult to understand but I think it was what he wanted, to die as he did, fighting to save his friends. Thorfinn never wanted to die in his bed, he told me that once. He wanted so much to go to Asgard, and a Viking can only do that if he dies in battle.'

'I thought you didn't believe in Asgard any more.'

'He believed in it, that's what mattered.' The wind ruffled Kari's cloak, and although flecks of rain blew into their faces, the sun suddenly appeared from behind the clouds. 'Look,' said Kari, pointing towards the mountains, where a great arch of many-coloured lights had appeared, directly behind Thorfinn's burial mound.

'It's the rainbow bridge,' Elf said. 'Isn't it? The rainbow bridge to Asgard . . .'

Kari smiled and squeezed her hand. 'That's right,' he said. 'He's gone now.'

They spent the night at a nearby farmstead, and next morning they left for the summer farm in Godaland.

They rode back around the northern flanks of the glaciers, taking the same route they had followed after fleeing from the summer farm. The mountain called 'Odin's cauldron' was once again quiet and still, sleeping coldly and silently under its mantle of snow and ice. There was no sign that it was capable of the fury they had seen.

'I wonder how long it'll be before it erupts again . . .' Olaf murmured, as he looked up towards the cloud-covered summit of the mountain.

'Never, I hope,' Elf said, shuddering, but Olaf shook his head.

'There's a fire in there somewhere,' he said. 'Right inside the mountain. We'll go and bathe in the hot pool when we get to the summer farm next year. If the water's still hot then the fire is still alight. Something has to heat the water, doesn't it?'

At mid-evening time they finally reached the summer farm. As soon as they dismounted, Elf took off Freyfaxi's halter and the pony immediately bounded across the turf, neighing with excitement, to rejoin the other ponies. Elf and Olaf ran up to the farmhouse, where they had a wild and noisy reunion with Hildi and the other girls. Frekki danced around them, barking and jumping up to lick their faces. It was a real homecoming. Elf had no idea that everybody would be so happy to see them returned safely, and she was weeping with joy. Even old Unn came out and embraced the pair of them.

I really belong somewhere, Elf thought happily. *I've come home.*

Next day the great round-up of all the sheep and ponies began. Asjolf and several of the other men had already ridden up from the home farm, and all day long Elf and Olaf roamed the mountains with them, helping to bring the animals down into the valley. The bleating flocks of sheep and ewes were driven into the stone sheepfolds, where they were sorted out according to their brand-marks, and returned to their owners. Elf and Olaf were very happy to find that Eyvind was among the crowd of shepherds who were busy counting in their flocks at the sheepfolds.

'Don't forget that you owe me a ride on that pony of yours,' he said to them, as they set off into the fells to round up more of the sheep.

After five glorious days, only six of Sigurd's sheep were still missing, and by the time they found them it was already dark.

'Only one more night at the summer farm,' Kari said. He was enjoying the autumn round-up as much as anybody. 'Then it's back to gloomy old Thorolfsfell for the winter.'

'Until next year,' Elf said, patting Freyfaxi's head.

'And the year after that,' added Olaf.

They were walking now, leading their ponies across a rocky pavement just below the glacier. Olaf had chosen the pony called Gullfaxi, his old companion of the midnight riding lessons. Ahead of them, the six plump sheep hurried on, bleating happily and padding the frosty ground.

'Look!' Kari exclaimed suddenly, pointing up into the sky. Elf craned her neck heavenwards.

'Oh!' she gasped out loud. 'What is it? It's so beautiful . . .'

Across the dome of the sky hung a great arch of radiant light, gleaming across the glaciers and extending northwards across the mountains of the interior.

'Look! Look!' Elf cried. The lights began bending and rippling across the sky, like a shining ribbon blowing in a soft breeze. Then, quite suddenly, the sky seemed to explode in a blaze of coloured lines, green, mauve, red and yellow, shimmering and dancing until they formed columns of shining colours.

'I wonder what it is?' Olaf murmured. 'There must be a reason for it.' Elf turned to look at him.

'Oh, Olaf, you are funny,' she said. Her eyes shone with the reflections of the many coloured lights. 'It's a sign. A sign for us. Because we've come through everything.'

'No it isn't, it's just happening.'

Kari interruped their argument. 'They are called the lights of Elfheim,' he said. 'You can only see them in the far north of the world. They say there is a great hall beyond the heavens, where the light-elves live. It is made all of gold, and sometimes, especially in the autumn and the spring, we can see the light shining from its windows.'

Even Freyfaxi had stopped, and was staring up into the sky. For a moment, nobody spoke.

Elf looked down from the splendour in the sky, and smiled at Kari. 'It's so beautiful', she said again.

Kari smiled too. 'If you listen very carefully,' he said, 'you can hear the elves singing . . .'

They listened. They could hear the wind moaning across the crags, and from far away in a remote valley, the shrill yapping of the arctic foxes as they moved south in search of food.

'I can't hear anything,' Olaf muttered.

'I can,' said Elf.

Still arguing about it, they hurried down into the valley, leaving the mountains, until the next year, to the foxes, the frost giants, and the trolls.